What people are saying about
A Midlife Voyage to Transformation . . .

Donna Daniell chose a healing journey that shifted her life. This book is an intimate account of her transformation in midlife to self-awareness and what moved her to create a roadmap for other women on the journey of life to achieve inner peace, wholeness, and authenticity. This is an inspiring story.

> –TONI HERBINE-BLANK, RN, MA, IFS Trainer and coauthor of
> *Intimacy from the Inside Out, Courage and Compassion in Couple Therapy*

As the story of Donna's personal and therapist career paths unfold, her intensely personal memoir evolves into something more universal, with insights for all of us.

> –DAVID LOY, PH.D; author of *Ecodharma: Buddhist Teachings for the Ecological Crisis*

Donna has given us an unmeasurable gift. Her voice serves as a much needed trail guide for women everywhere as we navigate and evolve through our own midlife journeys. Through her courageously shared memoir, she invites us to walk with her through the raw and real life struggles that accompany motherhood, marriage, divorce, menopause, and the inevitable deaths of our loved ones. Not only are her stories profoundly relatable, they also spark spiritual inquiry that invites a personal and collective rebirth. Donna culminates her book by inviting us to embrace our own personal healing path, to find our inner *Wisewoman* by introducing us to her program for women in midlife which integrates mindfulness and Internal Family Systems, two of the most valuable tools for personal transformation.

> –DR. ARIELLE SCHWARTZ, PH.D; psychologist, yoga teacher, and author of many books including *The Post-Traumatic Growth Guidebook*

Donna's story is an example of what we can realize in our lives when we take responsibility for our own personal healing. Choosing to find a path of healing from multiple traumas that afflict us in the 21st century is something we can all pursue for ourselves, but sometimes we need guidance to find it. Through reading Donna's stories and struggles and her exploration of the healing tools of mindfulness and IFS, individuals can get real guidance about how they can learn to use trauma healing tools to bring a spiritual rebirth to themselves and into their families, communities and beyond—a powerfully hopeful pathway toward healing our world.

–KRITEE (KANKO), PH.D; Zen priest and meditation teacher; Climate scientist, Environmental Defense Fund; Cofounder, Rocky Mountain Ecodharma Retreat Center

Donna has inspired me in this memoir about her journey of self-discovery and healing. These stories of her raw struggles through parenting, divorce and depression show women how to keep moving past our fears to claim our authentic selves waiting there—a "must read" for midlife women wanting to use these healing tools to navigate their own journeys to self-empowerment.

–CAROL GARNAND

A Midlife Voyage to
Transformation

A Midlife Voyage to
Transformation

Donna Roe Daniell

MINDFUL BOOKS
Longmont, CO

A Midlife Voyage to Transformation
Donna Roe Daniell
Copyright ©2021 by Donna Roe Daniell

ISBN: 978-1-7368497-0-5 paperback
ISBN: 978-1-7368497-1-2 e-book
Library of Congress Control Numner: 2021906832

Mindful Books
Longmont, CO 80504

Editing by Melanie Mulhall, Dragonheart
www.DragonheartWritingandEditing.com
Cover and interior design by Bob Schram, Bookends Design
www.bookendsdesign.com

First Edition
Printed in the United States of America

Contents

Introduction   1

1. Lost at Sea   11

2. Finding a Mooring   19

3. Divorce When You Don't See It Coming   35

4. Single Mom   49

5. New Ways of Being   59

6. Reclaiming Family   69

7. Befriending My Parts   77

8. My Fierce and Wise Feminine Parts   85

9. Starting Over   97

10. Finding Joy Within   113

11. Riding the Waves of Midlife   123

12. Grief as a Guide   137

13. Building My Self-Compassion Container   147

14. Choosing Me   157

15. Fear and Awakening   165

16. Answering the Call to Authenticity   185

17. The Deep Dive through Grief   195

18. Rebirthing the New You   207

Afterword   219

Acknowledgments   225

About the Author   229

Introduction

AS I DESCENDED SLOWLY DOWN Mt. Kilimanjaro in Tanzania, Africa, on day seven of our climb, I chose to make it a solitary journey and let my summit expedition group go ahead to the bottom. I wanted to savor my last day like it was my personal pilgrimage. I had worked hard for the past week on the mountain, and I wanted to relax.

As I journeyed down, I met many of the climbers who, just like me, had made the six-day climb and had completed the 19,456 foot summit in the wee hours of dawn the previous day. My eight-mile downward trudge was a victory walk for me. The previous day had been grueling, especially when we summitted, and I was taking my time to take in the interesting personalities of my fellow climbers. I was engulfed by the sweet smell of blooming azaleas coming from the edge of the trail, so familiar to me from growing up in Florida, and it settled me into my body and heart. Gratitude swelled up inside me. I glanced over at the purplish-pink blossoms with the sun splashing on their glorious color. Every day, that magical mountain brought some new and uniquely different natural delight to explore.

In that moment, I heard feet pounding down the trail toward me. A man who appeared to be running alone ahead of his porter passed me. "How can you run down this mountain?" I called out. "My hips are killing me!"

He looked back at me and stopped in his tracks. Then he walked back up the trail to where I was standing and looked at me in a way I couldn't turn away from with a pair of very deep-set, penetrating dark eyes that pulled me right into his intensity. Those very eyes had caught my attention on day two of the climb when we were all coming out of our rain gear after being stuck in pouring rain for three hours. He and his Turkish friends had been singing under the huge waterfalls that poured down the rock outcroppings, and he looked up at me as our group passed by. They were getting a wonderful, refreshing shower. My body longed to be under that waterfall, but maybe not with those men.

Our eyes met one other time as we were all struggling to get a hold on the precariously crowded Barranco Wall on day three. I didn't think much about it then because I was focused on getting to the top of the 19,456 foot mountain, but I did notice him.

Now he came even closer, looked at me more intensely, and asked me my name. "Donna, your hips are holding the pain of so many—those you have listened to and given your support. You are giving out so much love. I can feel it in you now."

I wondered how he knew I was a therapist even on Kilimanjaro —my give-back trip to Africa. How did this part of me show? I asked his name.

"Halmouth," he said. It was a Turkish name. "I work with the healing love of Mary, Mother of Jesus. Did you know that you also exude that essence? Do you know of Mary's love?"

I felt a powerful spirit of love coming from him, as if he were a true embodiment of Jesus himself. It felt like everything I had read and learned about Jesus' love growing up in a Presbyterian church. He talked of Mary, Mother of Jesus, and how he carried her love and the love of great healers. He spoke of knowing the path of healers and the intensity of their love and compassion.

He spoke of his work as an osteopath and a healer, but I honestly couldn't follow all of what he was saying because his essence was so mysterious and so much love poured out of him. I just felt a warm, comforting love coming toward me, encircling me, and it was more powerful than the words he was saying. My heart opened more deeply to take it in.

He continued talking about Mary, Mother of Jesus, and her love as a way to bring things back to the compassionate healer archetype that he was seeing in me. It was a way of seeing me I had never before experienced. He saw my heart open for so many, and he saw my woundedness, my struggle to love myself fully, and the suffering it had caused me. I had never been seen and validated so totally. I noticed another feeling—a surge of self-appreciation coming forward that felt almost like self-trust.

He clearly had something to say to me, and it felt like he had been working up to one particular thing he wanted to say. "Donna, love yourself first, and great love will follow!" Then he flashed his intense eyes at me with deep sincerity, and he was gone. His long legs moved quickly down the trail, and all I could see was Halmouth's loaded-down porter following him quietly and reverently.

I slowly continued down the steep trail, as if in a trance, feeling that Halmouth's unique message was somehow my call to learn to love myself as fully as I could and that it would guide me to what was coming next. I had been in a major transition since my divorce two years earlier. But how could I learn to love myself more? And what could it guide me toward?

Even after he was gone, I felt his self-love surrounding me and infiltrating my soul. A warm compassion and caring for himself and others permeated my being. It was powerful.

Then I got it. Halmouth was role modeling for me how to work with compassion within myself and with others in a more balanced way and how to give love to myself as much as I gave it out to others. He was also helping me learn how to trust and love who I was right in that moment, messy but alive and present as I struggled with it all. He was showing me how to wrap a blanket of compassion around myself and hold myself with love, just as he did.

As I reflected on his messages upon my return from that trip, I kept being curious about what was keeping me from loving myself just as I was. I was still suffering from choosing to leave a marriage and feeling like a failure. How could I accept my woundedness in a way that allowed me to be more fully who I was in the moment? Wasn't the trip and the climb all about focusing on my strengths? Somehow I was not letting myself feel my goodness and strengths because the pain was so strong. I had consciously pushed myself physically to have adventure because that was where I knew I could expand and grow myself more. I was good at pushing myself physically. It was one of my gifts. But I didn't know how to put myself back together with all the pain and fear inside me. Was I loving all of me, even my grieving parts? Why did I need Halmouth's message to wake me up?

I began to dig deeper into myself. How did I get to the place of facing my fears of a lifetime to be able to climb Kilimanjaro? Something had been shifting big time over the past three years and I was going to learn more about what it was. At sixty-four, I had consciously created a ripe and terrifying moment for myself without knowing why. I began to break free from all the restraints of being a woman that I had probably both bought into and challenged my whole life. Because of my pain and fear, I was cracking open inside and feeling the path of a deeper self-awakening that was already happening. Some spirit within was guiding me from the inside out, and Halmouth had been that spirit embodied. I could feel the tingling warmth of Halmouth's self-love and compassion growing inside me. The seed had been planted.

From that moment on, I have been manifesting the path of self-love and self-compassion that Halmouth laid out for me.

Midlife, the ages of thirty-nine to sixty-five, has been for me an adventure in finding authenticity, healing, and the integration of the many parts or aspects of me that make up my wholeness. But mostly, it's been about finding a way to trust myself and be who I truly am, to live my truth. As you read my story, specifically the major transitions I experienced between thirty-nine and sixty-five, I hope you see yourself in your own challenges and see a path of resilience and hope for yourself similar to what I have found. I have chosen to write about these events because they have been instrumental in teaching me so much about myself, have grown me into the transformed woman I am today, and have healed me into a sense of wholeness from my brokenness.

I had to drop into my old pattern of letting others tell me who I was and what I wanted many times before I could pull myself out of it. Growing up a girl in the 1960s in Florida, I was fed fear and sexism, though I was very privileged. I became a tomboy and an intellectual rather than a southern belle. I chose to develop my masculine traits first. It was all about playing a part to show the world something rather than learning how to be me inside. I was a chameleon.

I had to leave the Floridian world and move to Colorado when I was twenty-four to discover who I really was. And then it took depression, death, and divorce to jump-start my growth process. That was the silver lining: From learning to embrace my brokenness, my fears, my struggles, and my losses and going down into the pain, I stumbled on a gentler and very loving me deep inside. I knew she was there, but she was very sad and lost for a long time, trying to make life work.

This story is also about relationships: my relationship with my mother, my relationship with my son, my relationships with my two husbands, and most importantly, the relationship I learned to develop with myself. How do relationships help us find ourselves, our wholeness? When do we need to move out into ourselves to find our truth? When do we need to move into a relationship with others to get mirrored and loved? How does that help us find our truth too? These are questions I have pondered my whole life because of the struggle I had as a baby trying to get the connection and attunement I needed and wanted in my attachment with my mother. I had to find healthy connections, and I had to learn to start with my connection with myself.

We women are taught to be attuned to others. Learning to attune to ourselves is the key to moving down the midlife path to transformation or rebirth.

This story is about some of those important connections I had and still have in my life—those relationships where the dance of attunement and mirroring is powerful—and how we can learn from the reflections of our friends, sisters, partners, and other women on the path. How do we help each other differentiate and grow in relationships? How do we hold each other back from our own awakening?

I've learned about healthy attunement, which involves attunement to self at the same time you are attuning to another. It's a spiraling flow back and forth with each other that takes some practice. It can be difficult in intimate relationships if each partner is not conscious and aware of themselves in the process.

And it can be hard to master when we parent challenging children. As women, sometimes our relationships—including relationships with our families—can hold us back from finding our personal awakening. How do we take responsibility for and chart our own paths as women? How do we let go and finally find our authentic path?

This is a story about how I got there on Kilimanjaro, where I was helping five young African women get to the top of a mysterious mountain they were told they couldn't climb. I now support women and girls all over the world in learning and growing who they are because it takes all of us to help find our voices and our true openheartedness.

It wasn't until I lost my favorite sister in a car accident when I was thirty-two that I learned to start paying attention to what was happening inside me and began exploring the feelings within me that had both scared and delighted me. I had to miss my sister's adoration to realize I had to replace it with learning to care for myself better and appreciate my energy and gifts, which had been disregarded, judged, or poorly mirrored by my parents so early. I had adored my baby sister Marjorie as much as she had adored me, and her death was the beginning of my first major midlife transition.

This is also a story about the underside of grief, of what happens after you go deeply into your feelings of grief and loss. After resisting grief in many ways, I learned to slow down and begin to feel the sadness and all the other feelings I'd been suppressing. And just when I thought I had it all figured out, the complexity of more grief hit me. The mystery of the underside of that grief was that once I allowed myself to go into it, I found it to be a huge blessing: a rebirthing of love and life's creativity and a reclaiming of parts of myself I didn't know were there. That happened more than once after a difficult disconnection

and/or death in some form: after my first divorce, as I was settling into my second marriage; as my mother was lingering in
her wheelchair; after my mother died; and again, later. There I
found the unmet longing that knows what you desire deeply
inside, mixed with all the sadness.

Through many transitions, I found that if I followed that
longing over the bridge into the unknown, I found a deeper me,
a connection to myself I was longing for and couldn't find until
then. That rebirthing came with deep diving into myself, and
the transformed me is my Wisewoman. I love her so much now,
and I'm letting her out because she has so much to share with
you.

This story is coming to you directly from my Wisewoman,
and it is about my voyage, but even though the details of the
voyage are my own, I believe many women go through their
own midlife voyage with transformation as its destination. This
voyage is about learning to ride the larger waves of midlife that
come bigger and faster as we age instead of being knocked down
by them, and it has five stages: Lost at Sea; Finding a Mooring;
Deep Diving; Rebirthing; and the New You.

I gained the tools and experience to be more resilient and
alive, and you can too. Those tools have taught me to live in
the present more and drop deeper into my softer Divine
Feminine knowing—the heart space—and hang out there. It is
a soft, self-compassionate place, sweet and kind, and it is filled
with self-trust, longing, love, truth, self-forgiveness, and deep
connection. I hope this story of my healing midlife voyage can
help you find your own midlife transformation and set sail to
this softer, gentler New You.

From that place, that deep heart connection with ourselves
and others, I believe we can lead others on the path to what's
next for us and all living creatures on this planet. I believe that

when we heal ourselves deeply and release our inner trauma and pain through deep grieving, we are ready and open to step forward into our new role of healing the world and our species. I hope you find your path of inner healing through deep waters so you can come forth as the mermaid, transformed and ready, as I am.

Let's join hands and heal ourselves now.

Chapter One

Lost at Sea

IT ALL BEGAN WITH A PERFECT twelve-hour, no drug delivery after a very healthy and wonderful, but unbelievably lonely, pregnancy. My birth plan had worked. My husband Peter was at my side and had even videotaped the birth. We felt like a team. It had gone so well that the doctor released me from the hospital that evening after the baby was six hours old. I was a super-achiever, so I agreed with him, thinking I was a champ.

"It was just like running a marathon," Peter said. We had run marathons separately, but we trained together. I could go home for sure. We both felt prepared as we left the hospital.

Our son Julian was seven pounds, three ounces at birth, and he did okay until he received circumcision. Afterward, he was fussy and not really starting to breastfeed, even though I held him to my breast. My colostrum was not coming in and I was exhausted, but because I had a superbly successful birth, I got to go home.

That first night, Julian cried loudly and unconsolably almost all night, so I got no sleep. He was clearly hungry and trying to suck, but my breasts were not yet producing. I finally got something into him in the morning, and I was grateful because I wanted to breastfeed him.

I called my doctor and asked for a nursing specialist to come out, but it took three days for her to materialize. In the meantime, I called one of my closest friends, and she came over with meals and her mother. With their home-cooked food and nurturing support, I was able to breastfeed more and get a bit of rest when Julian napped. I was exhausted for the next several days, but when I picked up my crying baby and brought him to my heart, the soothing connection between us filled my body, which was otherwise struggling with fear and anxiety. I alternated between *wondering* if I could actually be a mother to this child and *knowing* that I could.

I also struggled with the knowledge that Peter hadn't wanted me to get pregnant, was ambivalent through the pregnancy, and wasn't really helping with Julian's care. It appeared that it was going to all be up to me. I reflected on the night Julian was conceived. I was using the rhythm method of birth control, and that night, New Year's Eve, Peter agreed to try to conceive, knowing that I was fertile. But when I told him I was pregnant several weeks later, he seemed distraught and distant. Over the six years we had talked about having a family, Peter showed ambivalence and confusion about it, so even though I had been ready to start a family, I was never clear if he was.

In many ways, it was perplexing that Peter couldn't see and feel what I did with Julian: the newness and even foreignness of this tiny being I loved; the sweetness of his smell; how solid and real he felt in my arms, but also how fragile he seemed; the emotions he triggered in me, all the way down to my root chakra. I loved being a mom, even though it was the biggest challenge I had faced in my life.

I felt I could have the baby or have my husband, but not both, and I wondered why it had to be one or the other. At times, Peter looked at me as if he didn't know me—or worse, as if I were an alien and someone he despised. I felt pulled between my connection with my husband of ten years and my connection with my baby. But ultimately, I resigned myself to the need to pull inward, not fight Peter, and focus my attention on the baby. There was only so much energy I had to muster, and the baby needed me. It occurred to me that my husband might be feeling I didn't have any energy for him, but there was little I could do about it at the moment. And he wasn't rising to the occasion.

In desperation, I called my mother for help, and she flew in from Florida the next day. For the next week, I focused on trying to get enough food into Julian while trying to get myself on a schedule of breastfeeding that allowed some rest for me. I was dropping deeper into fear and the feeling of being lost, and my mom's presence was helpful. She bathed the baby for me, went to his first checkup with me, was with me when I asked the doctor for sleeping pills, and helped me get Julian onto supplemental formula. All the while, I fought an incredible reluctance to take on the job of being a new mother. I felt I had to face that fear, but I was too weak and too lost to get on top of it. When it was time for my mom to return to Florida, I felt stronger, but I was still not sleeping much.

I hoped Peter would take my mom's place in some way. Two weeks later, when Peter's parents came to visit, I was barely holding on, and Peter had not stepped up to help me. I could see that he was not only lost like me but frozen in the way he talked to his folks. He didn't even call them ahead of time to warn them.

As soon as they came through the door and took the baby from me to hold, I walked into my bedroom and packed my bags. I was going to take Julian to Florida on the next flight, which meant that Peter's parents would only have a few hours with Julian. I didn't care. I had never shown that side of myself to my mother-in-law, but it somehow felt justified. I knew I was depressed. I knew Peter was unable to help me, and I actually wanted her to see that. I was heading to Florida where I could truly get rested and comforted.

What I didn't realize was that I was going right back into the very environment that had spawned patterns I had been working hard to release. I had left Florida in 1976, two years after graduating from college, and had moved to Colorado on my own. I'd met Peter in Steamboat Springs the following year. I was now a therapist, and I knew that we always regress when we go home, no matter when it is, no matter how much personal work we have done. But this was an emergency, and I needed my family. My adult self would have to step back and allow my younger and very fragile self to seek the comfort of home because my son and I needed help.

And being in Florida did help a bit. I'd developed a nursing routine that was working using my own and supplemental milk, and my three-week-old baby was finally getting enough to eat. But I was still not sleeping. When my mother asked me how I was one morning, I was feeling grumpy and helpless, and I gave her my truth. "I maybe slept four hours. I'm not sure. The sleeping pills are almost gone, and each of them only lasts four hours. My doctor in Boulder was hesitant to give me enough."

I was still exhausted, and while it was good to have my mom's help, she seemed to be taking over my job a bit. I decided to tell her what I had been turning over and over in my mind when I wasn't sleeping at night. I was feeling more and more lost and disconnected from my body and from Julian, and I was afraid I was failing as a mother. I was feeling both helpless and lost trying to take care of Julian. Displaced. Dysfunctional.

The previous spring I had completed my master's degree in social work, and I was studying for my licensing exam. I'd had a full-time job in a residential treatment center before Julian's birth, and I planned to return to that job three months following it. The trained social worker part of me was functioning well. She lived in my brain and mind, and she was loud and clear: I was depressed.

"Mom, I've got major depression. I know my symptoms from studying for my LCSW licensing exam. The major ones are depressed mood every day, most of the day, marked diminished interest or pleasure in almost all activities, insomnia or hypersomnia every day, psychomotor agitation nearly every day that is recognizable by others, feelings of worthlessness or excessive or inappropriate guilt, and diminished ability to think or make decisions. That was the criteria I memorized for my exam, and I've had five or more of the symptoms for at least two weeks."

In that moment, I was grateful for trusting my mind and the knowledge about depression I'd absorbed. Some of the anxiety eased, and I thought I might be finding a way out of the dark place I was in. "Mom, I need an appointment with a psychiatrist. I'm way depressed."

She looked shocked. "Donna, you really think you need that kind of help, dear?"

She had always been uncomfortable with my feelings, and her response was part of a pattern I knew well.

"Let me take over with Julian for a while, and you go to an exercise class today. That one we found should be around 10:00 a.m. You could get ready and get there easily today." She knew exercise was key for me to get my body balanced again.

I had actually discovered how important it was for me when I left Florida and moved to Colorado at twenty-four. My mother had paid attention to how much my athletic activities had served me in Steamboat Springs and how much more athletic I had become with Peter. But in true Mom style, she dismissed the intensity and emotional energy in my voice, which was meant to show the truth of what I was saying. I felt somewhat supported, but only halfway. It was as much as she could give. She did a good job at seeing the practical things I needed like exercise, but I needed more warmth and understanding when I was emotional. At least as an adult, I knew I could look for other people who might respond to me differently.

I recalled being teased in Latin class when I was in middle school and coming home distraught, talking really fast with lots of emotion. My mom just sat me down, and instead of listening to what I was saying, she told me what to feel and how to handle it. It was uncomfortable to be treated in that heavy-handed way, and I got more agitated. And yet I accepted her approach because I didn't know how to deal with my feelings. I learned to push aside my feelings with disgust and think through a strategy that didn't have anything to do with how I was feeling but was all about how I looked outwardly.

But in that moment of postpartum depression, I had amazing clarity. Mom's strategic approach was not serving me. I went downstairs to the dining room where my dad was having breakfast, sat down, and began talking to him in a way that must have sounded like pleading. "Dad, I need to see a doctor or a psychiatrist. I need to get some meds. An antidepressant. Do you know of anyone here I could see?"

He looked up at me and could see my earnestness and clarity. He had always been able to tune into me more than Mom and was listening for the intensity of the Donna he knew. It felt comforting to me. "Dr. Hatch is our family doctor. Do you remember him? He would be a good place to start. Would you like me to call his office and see if he can see you?"

"Yes, I remember him," I replied with relief. "Is he a family practice doc? Let's try that, Dad." I was happy I didn't have to explain anything more because he got it.

At Dr. Hatch's office that afternoon, I felt listened to. He immediately wrote me a prescription for antidepressants and sleep medications. My mother did the night feedings with Julian for another week while I slept through the nights and got rested. The antidepressant slowly began to help. I began to feel better with regular exercise and a little more sleep, and my body started relaxing into my new role as mother. I took over the night feedings and was able to sleep again after a few weeks of being on the antidepressant.

My body had held my truth, but it had needed my awareness and attention to show me *what* to do and then *do* it.

Peter flew down to Florida, and we spent a week working with therapists to process the challenges in our relationship and try to put our marriage back together. My parents were quite skeptical about whether Peter was actually seriously interested in working on the marriage. At one point, they asked me if I wanted to consider getting a divorce. I expected as much from my mom, considering she had never liked Peter, almost from the moment she met him.

Peter stayed positive with my mom while we were there, and I was grateful for that. I maintained a strong and hopeful front while feeling confused and exhausted inside. It wasn't until I got back home and started up a new routine with the baby that I could see I had gotten through the worst of it. I was a mother, and my life began to unfold around being both a new family therapist and a new mom.

Peter and I immediately started couples counseling, carrying baby Julian with us to the therapist's office in a portable bassinet. I also went to my own therapist to work through my postpartum depression more fully. I felt Peter and I had a long way to go to get our marriage back on track and I had a long way to go to get myself back on track, but I wanted to be successful as both a wife and a mother, and I was willing to do whatever was needed to accomplish that.

During my therapy process, I remembered that my family doctor, who had a more holistic approach than most, had suggested that meditation might help me. I decided to explore what meditation was and how it might help with depression. I looked at Transcendental Meditation, but as I read about that approach, I decided it wasn't for me, and I kept looking into other kinds of meditation. Ultimately, I found mindfulness-based stress reduction, or MBSR.

But before I was able to incorporate meditation into my life, I had to learn how depression happened in my body/mind. I began to seek answers by reading about depression and its causes, a scholarly approach that had gotten me ahead in life to that point. I also thought about how to teach what I was learning to people like me struggling with depression when I got my private practice started. When I went back to work, I decided it was important to structure my day to include time for self-care, which was the key takeaway from my study of managing depression. I wanted to get off the antidepressants, and I felt my depressed states had a lot to do with the dysregulated pattern of pushing hard and then crashing that I had carried into my adult life. Whenever I crashed, I got stuck trying to pull myself out of it because I had no idea what I was feeling.

That pattern had taken a toll on me when I lived in Steamboat Springs, and I knew I would not get out of depression if I repeated it now. Self-care meant taking time to exercise, rest, relax, and play. It was about finding a healthy balance in my life. I began to experiment with how much balance I could achieve with a new career, a new baby, and growing a family.

Chapter Two

Finding a Mooring

AS A KID GROWING UP in Florida, I got to ride in motorboats a lot. Whether it was on the freshwater lakes or the ocean, getting out your rope at the bow of your boat to moor your boat on the closest dock was an important safety skill. Finding a mooring was a priority that you thought about whenever you took your boat out, especially to new waters away from home.

One time when I was in junior high, two of my brothers and I were invited to go deep sea fishing with my dad in Islamorada near the Florida Keys. We seemed to go out farther than I had ever gone, and I was worried that we would get lost at sea. When Dad found the right spot, one where we would catch the fish running, he asked my brother, Bill, and me to throw out a huge anchor. I could hardly lift it and neither could he, but somehow we got it out of the boat and into the water. The anchor kept us from floating out to sea and out of our navigation sightings.

My early experiences on the water taught me that the key to finding your direction and safety in a boat was getting properly moored, and at the huge intersection of three major transitions in my life, I was finding a mooring by tying my ropes to the tools of self-care and life balance. They created the stability from which I could move forward. Therapy was helpful to process things, but to go forward, the tools became key. Being lost at sea for several months had taken a toll on me, but I was determined to move on in my life.

In my work life, I was launching a new career as a clinical social worker. Right out of graduate school, I'd gotten a great job as a new family therapist in training at a residential treatment center. After that, I took a position with a county program that offered individual and family therapy for at risk elementary school kids and their families on site at an elementary school. Those experiences with families suffering from neglect and abuse issues gave me valuable training and perspective to bring to healthier families.

As I began my family therapy practice, I mostly wanted to help mothers, maybe because of my own experience as a mother, but also because I felt that mothers had the most leverage and power in the family to create change when needed. I felt many mothers—myself included—needed extra support to do it all because in the 1980s and 1990s, we were blazing the trail of being working moms when many women were still choosing to be stay-at-home moms. I was struggling with how to do that while staying balanced and not dropping into depression again.

When Julian was two, I launched my private practice, part-time, in a shared office with other therapists. Getting to that point had been carefully calculated. Timing was everything. A couple of years later, I decided to get a shared office space with my colleague, Carol, who had also worked in a day treatment program before starting her private practice. We were both interested in helping families and kids, and we had similar training in family systems work. We joined an office with a couple who practiced in a suite we both liked.

Carol was a good choice for supporting me professionally because she was a few years ahead of me in building a full-time private practice in child and family therapy while raising a child. She was also hoping to have a second child in the near future. We shared the challenges of being working professionals with families. We also shared a love of being athletic outdoors, and we both had partners who loved doing athletic things in nature. Because of those commonalities, I felt she understood my feelings as a mom and some of my marital struggles. I didn't have many people with whom I could share my disappointments and joys with trying to get Peter engaged as a co-parent. We had some good supportive talks.

"Carol, how do you juggle it all?" I asked one day as we were waiting for our next clients. "You've been a mom for a while, but now you're thinking of having another child. When do you fit in time for you? I'm missing my runs and workout time with a four-year-old."

"I have a great husband who helps a lot, and I love my work," she replied. "What's it like for you?"

"I'm loving seeing families with little ones and helping them. I love being a family therapist, but I don't feel much support at home. Your husband seems so engaged with your daughter. And you want to have another baby? I can't fathom that with all I have on my plate right now."

"Yeah, this time we're doing in vitro since I can't seem to get pregnant. We'll see what happens. What do you think keeps Peter on the periphery? Do you guys talk about this?"

"I've tried until I'm blue in the face. You know, Julian has been tested and found to be in the 'gifted category.' I'd hoped Peter would see that as adults, we have some of the same gifted traits he has and that we have apparently passed some of those abilities on to him. But that hasn't even inspired him to get involved. Whether or not he gets that, knowing it is helping me learn more about myself and understand Julian better. We do great when we get outdoors and take Julian with us, but homelife is challenging. He just disappears."

"Well, I think you scare him because you're now a therapist. He sees how strong you are getting in your career. That's hard with all the changes in your life together now that you have a child."

"Yikes. Really? I don't think he even cares about what I'm doing. He seems indifferent and aloof, which is not good for our marriage."

Carol knew a bit about my relationship with Peter and its history, including our passion for the outdoors. Since our meeting in Steamboat Springs in 1979, Peter and I had been totally engaged in the outdoors together. He'd taught me to rock climb and he'd taught me mountain safety skills. I felt so much peace and solace in the mountains, and through our first ten years of marriage, right up until the time I got pregnant, we'd gone on ski, backpacking, and camping trips throughout Colorado. Nature was where we relaxed and rejuvenated on weekends and vacations.

Peter was a climbing guide and had been a member of the ski patrol, so he was an expert at being in nature. He understood how nature met a person where they were and challenged them to surpass their limitations because he had experienced it himself. For example, before we met, he learned to face and move beyond his fears and self-doubt by climbing mountains. He had climbed big peaks in the Canadian Rockies and had gone on other epic adventures. I felt we were soul mates learning tools to feel safe in nature, where we could totally experience our intensity and energy. He was my conduit to nature's healing, and I had made Colorado my home with him. But now we seemed to be in a new phase.

"Carol, how will you keep up your outdoor fun with more kids? You two really do a lot of hiking and skiing like us. Aren't you worried about how that will all change when you have more kids?"

I could see that Carol was a little upset by my questions, and I thought they had triggered some of her own fear about how having more than one child might impact her ability to maintain her life as it was with a thriving full-time private practice. We were both holding back, as if it were too much—too revealing and too unsettling—to share more about those subjects with each other.

"Dave is making good money at the bank. I can depend on him to support us through whatever happens. We've talked about the possibility of twins, and he's on board. We'll have to get a full-time nanny when I go back to work if we do have twins. It's a bit daunting to think about it all." She paused at that point and seemed to shift gears. "My client is arriving soon, so I need to get ready." The conversation was over for the time being, and we retreated to our work.

My office was set up so that my desk was near my Jungian-designed sand tray and figurines where I could work with a child alone or a parent and child together. That was adjacent to my bookcase. There was a large open seating area that had a loveseat and two black leather chairs on either side across the room. I had a closet nearby with all kinds of games, toys, and art supplies I could pull out or put away as needed with each family. On the wall across from the sofa was a huge glass that I used as a white board for writing and teaching. I was set up for all ages of kids and families.

From all the family systems master therapists in my trainings I'd learned that it was good to see the whole family in the room together, and my next clients were a family of young parents with children aged two and five. They were totally overwhelmed. They both worked outside the home, and their kids were in childcare.

I had a lot of families like them coming in on their insurance plans. It was hard to see enough of those families to make a decent wage with my part-time schedule and the fee the insurance paid me. Even though I was a Licensed Clinical Social Worker (LCSW), I still got only half of my fee through insurance. And it was always a challenge to balance my energy with the number of clients I could book within my days at the office. I had to pay full-time childcare for Julian too because the days I was not in my private practice office I worked at the Longmont Hospital Employee Assistance Program (EAP) program. But when I didn't think about the money I was making and focused on how good it felt to be helping the families, I was inspired to keep going. I wanted to help families get the tools they needed to make good decisions about parenting and schooling their kids and releasing their stress.

As I learned more from my own parenting of Julian, I was able to help parents learn how to advocate for their kid's needs in their school programs, find the right supplemental therapies and support, and set up good schedules for them at home to be more successful. Those tools, along with things I learned in training, became my toolbox for working with my client families of gifted and special needs kids. I connected with other therapists like me, doctors, occupational therapists, speech therapists, and others working with special needs and gifted children, and we formed a network of resources for the families of those kids.

The network was also a great support for me personally and professionally because I was in the thick of challenges with Julian. One afternoon I got a phone call from Dede at Julian's new preschool, Mapleton Montessori, where we had placed him a week earlier. "I need to talk to you about a situation we have right now with Julian," she said. "He's just climbed the fence around the playground, and I'm concerned about why he's so anxious here. Could you come by soon and help him with this?"

I was a little alarmed. "Is he okay? What do you mean, he's climbed the fence?"

"He got upset by something at recess and just walked over to the ten-foot fence and started climbing it. We were afraid he would actually climb out of the playground, so we stopped him."

Luckily, I had seen all my clients for the day, but that kind of emergency was my greatest challenge. It was why I chose to go into private practice instead of another kind of social work. I could arrange my hours and move clients around as I needed to make my family life work. Sometimes, though, that juggling carried the burden of holding the emotional container for everyone but me. And it wasn't good for building a business.

That day I left the office and headed over to Mapleton Montessori as soon as I could. I was opening a Boulder office so I could be closer to my home and Julian's school, but I hadn't started seeing clients there yet. As I got into my car, my mind raced. We'd just gotten Julian settled at his new preschool, and I was afraid we'd have to move him again. I tried to settle myself down by turning on some music as I drove, and I decided to *not* call Peter because I knew he wouldn't be happy and I didn't need his negativity. I was trying to include him in all our decisions, but I didn't want to include him until I had more of a handle on what was happening. When I got to the school office, Julian was playing checkers with Dede. I greeted them and asked who was winning. "Julian, of course," Dede said. "Have a seat. He's about to knock me out of this game, as you can see. He's really a wizard! Wow!"

I sat down and calmed myself with a few conscious deep breaths, feeling a little less stressed as I saw Julian getting the positive attention he needed after whatever had happened. I was impressed with Dede's connection to Julian and her true caring for him. Even after such a short time, she could see his gifts. That was promising. The game ended with Julian's last move. He smiled over at me and then came closer.

At four, I'd moved him into this larger preschool because his Waldorf home preschool teacher could no longer handle his activity level. She had six kids, and he was the most adventurous of them. He'd pushed the boundaries with her, especially at nap time. I knew our time there was limited, but it had been comforting for us both to have such a great Waldorf experience. I learned a lot from her about how to be calmer, and he loved both the outdoor activities at her farm and making so many fun things. It had worked well until it didn't. Then I searched for the right preschool and found Mapleton Montessori. I was impressed with Dede and her caring staff. And I thought Julian would thrive with the Montessori setup that kept him structured and stimulated.

Dede turned to Julian. "Julian, can you tell your mom what happened today?"

He looked down. "I got scared and climbed the fence."

"What caused you to get scared, sweetie?" I asked, looking for any information in his face.

He didn't have an answer and just looked at me and Dede sheepishly.

I put my hand on his leg and said, "It's important to know why you got scared so we can help you feel safe again. We all want you to feel safe here. It's not okay to climb the fence because that is really dangerous. You could get hurt if you fall."

Dede chimed in. "I want to help you feel safe here, Julian, because I really like you and all the kids do too. Will you promise not to do that again?"

Looking down, Julian nodded his head. Then he looked at me as if he needed me to know something he couldn't express.

"Okay," I said. "We'll talk more about it and see if we can figure out more at home tonight. Do you want to stay and play more, or shall we go home?"

Julian grabbed my hand. "Mom, before we go, can I show you my picture?"

"Sure, where is it?"

Dede smiled, and we all walked down the stairs to his classroom to see his drawings and other artwork. He grabbed a picture and put it behind his back so I couldn't see it.

Dede smiled knowingly at him and said to me, "He painted a special picture for you."

Julian showed me his picture of a yellow star with a glowing multicolored hexagon flowing out like sunbeams from the edges of it. "Mom, this is you. You are my shining star!"

I pulled him closer and hugged him. Time seemed suspended in that moment. I knew we both needed moments like that. Then we walked out holding hands as we headed to the car.

As I entered the house, I signaled to Peter that we needed to talk. He was reading a textbook at the desk in his office, which was adjacent to the kitchen. It looked like he was prepping his new class. As a new adjunct professor at CU, he was excited about joining the speech communication faculty and teaching the big introductory speech/communication classes. He had only completed his PhD a year before I finished my master's degree in social work, and he'd had a few part-time positions around the area until the position at CU. Both of us had received our degrees from DU, a plan we had discussed before leaving Steamboat Springs together in 1981 after deciding we were ready to grow up and leave our beloved paradise, which was known as Ski Town USA.

I made sure Julian was settled with a snack and was occupied away from hearing distance. Then I headed into Peter's office to talk, dropped into the chair in front of his desk, and began picking at my cuticles as I started to talk. "Julian had an incident at Mapleton today." My cuticle picking was a sure sign of worry, and the habit had been with me for a long time. Peter was irritated by it.

"There you go again, picking at your nails. Can you stop that?" Peter said without looking up from the textbook.

I felt criticized, as I had growing up by my mother. I looked up at him, trying to get his full attention by searching with my eyes for his. "Look, you aren't around, and there's a lot that happens with our kid. I have reason to be worried. I don't know where we can place him next if it doesn't work out for him at Mapleton Montessori." I couldn't seem to get his attention and raised my voice. "You know how many changes we've had to make so far with his childcare and education!" I ended with a loud sigh.

"What happened?" he asked, finally present. He put down his book and looked up.

I shared the whole incident with him except for the picture of the star. That was something I got to savor just for myself. As I spoke, I could see Peter's expression turn from curiosity to something that looked like disgust.

"Julian needs to learn how to be in a school and follow the rules!" Peter said in a harsh, authoritarian, angry tone. His brow was tense and his eyes were squinted, but the handsome, weath-ered angle of his jaw I loved was still there. "He's a good kid, really," he added more softly.

Then he seemed to just drop into a separate reality, and I couldn't bring him back no matter what I said. He'd left me emotionally as fast as he'd arrived, and I could feel what had become a deadened conduit between us.

I realized I had already decided what to do. I didn't need Peter's input because, as usual, it just dragged me down to share it all with him. On and off for several months, I'd felt it was all up to me. Peter seemed to disappear whenever Julian had behavior issues.

"I'm going to consult with my gifted kids support network," I said. "I'm sure someone will have an idea about what I should do to help Julian with this." With that, I walked out of his office and headed to the kitchen to make dinner.

Trying to team up with Peter was a constant struggle, but I wasn't ready to see the truth of how detached Peter had become. While I might have wished I no longer cared, I still wanted Peter to be with me in our new chapter of parenting. I believed I just had to stay positive and forward thinking because I had a wonderful little kid to raise. And I hoped things would get better when he got into elementary school.

We had enrolled Julian in a ski program for four-year-olds, and the next morning we drove up Boulder Canyon to the small ski area known as Eldora near the town of Nederland. Julian was excited about going on his own to ski with his peers because he was already pretty confident about his skiing abilities. This was primarily due to Peter's careful teaching on the bunny slope over the past winter. Peter had taken him up the lift, put Julian between his skis, and helped him learn to master the wedge at first. Then he put his climbing harness on him, connected him to a rope, and guided him down the slope so he could begin to feel his own mastery on his skis. Peter had engendered in Julian a love for skiing, and that made me very happy.

That morning we all planned to go up together. Julian would go with his group and Peter and I would get some fun ski time together at the Nordic center where we had raced and skied together for several years before Julian was born. Since I loved being active so much, Peter had encouraged me to train and enter ski races in the winter and run and do triathlons in the summer. Because it was a great way for me to deal with my intensity and high energy, being an athlete was one of my tools for balancing myself. Our best athletic adventures together involved cross-country ski racing, which we did every winter weekend until we got pregnant.

The plan that day at Eldora allowed all of us to get what we wanted. But of course, it depended on the weather and whether Julian felt safe with his instructors and the weather. As usual, the wind was brutal as we drove up the canyon. I was concerned about whether they would take the kids out in that wind. If they didn't, Peter and I would have to change our plans, and I was worried how Peter would react. No matter how much I wanted us to be a family, Peter still held back from family opportunities to be together doing what we loved. I saw that day's outing not only as great family time, but also as another chance to help Julian feel good about the things he did well.

We parked and headed to the Trek program building with all our gear. Julian was downhill skiing and we were Nordic skiing, and I thought it was great that both options were so close together at this local ski area. Julian saw his friend Alden from our neighborhood and grabbed my hand, pulling me closer to Alden and his parents. I was glad that Alden was there too. We got in the registration line behind them, and I talked to Alden's mom while waiting to be checked in. Peter was quiet, standing back out of the line holding our skis and waiting. Finally, we moms got the kids checked in, and I went over to talk to Julian's instructors.

"Will you be taking the kids out in the wind? Julian should be okay because he's used to this place. He's got an extra jacket, snacks, and lunch in his backpack."

Julian stood next to me listening. "Mom, I want to ski with Alden. Can we do that?"

"I'm sure you two will be skiing together," I replied and turned toward Peter, wanting his help getting Julian settled with the teachers. He was looking away and talking with Alden's dad.

Frustrated about having to do it all, I turned to the instructors and mentioned that Julian wanted to be with Alden. Then I saw that they were moving the kids out with their skis to get started. Julian and Alden were engaged and looked happy. I waved good-bye and headed over to Peter to walk over to the Nordic Center. It looked like Alden's parents were heading out to ski together too.

As we put on our skate skis and headed up the ski trail to the trees, I felt torn. I wanted to have a plan to check in with Julian because it was his first day out alone, but I didn't even get a chance to say that because I felt rushed by Peter to go out and ski with him.

The wind was challenging and my skis slipped a bit on the path where the wind had scoured it, but the path became less icy and my endorphins kicked in. Warm feelings poured in on top of my worry. I wanted to ski with Peter, but I also wanted us to ski as a family. We'd put Julian in a program so we could ski together as we had before he was born, not knowing if he would like the program or if he would get upset by the wind. I wanted to know how he was doing and check on him.

As I felt anger flaring up, I pushed more into my right heel, pushing the ski forward. It felt too challenging to bring up my feelings with Peter. Instead, I focused on having fun with him so I could at least feel some connection with him as outdoor athletes. That had always been the glue for our relationship, but with Julian, I wasn't sure how it was going to be going forward.

I focused on my love of ski skating as I glided around the trees following Peter briskly. The rhythm of the kick and glide was so soothing to me that I finally dropped into gratitude. I felt grateful for the beauty of the aspen trees and the deep experience of nature I was having. I loved the warmth of the sensations that were pouring through my body as I skied, waking me up and rejuvenating my energy. Doing that kind of athletic activity on the weekends was helping me stay balanced with my work and my parenting, and it was also helping me move out of my depression.

When we returned from our ski, Julian and Alden were kicking a soccer ball around in the kids' program room. It looked like they were the last two kids to be picked up.

"Hi, Julian. Hi, Alden. Did you guys have a good day?"

"Yup," was all I got from Julian as he looked up briefly but kept his focus on the ball. It was the best focus on the soccer ball I had seen from him that soccer season. But since Alden was on his team, the one-on-one connection was helping him maintain focus.

I turned back to see the instructor talking to Peter and Alden's parents arriving. "How did Julian do? Was the wind a problem?" I asked, jumping in.

"No problem, Mrs. Daniell. He was a delight to be with today! Skied out in front with me, and the wind was on and off but not a problem. I hope you'll be here all winter for this program. He's a perfect fit."

I needed that positive report after a week of preschool challenges. On the way home, Peter was able to acknowledge Julian's success a tiny bit, but I still wanted him to praise Julian and encourage him more. I figured the instructor had Julian ski with him not only to separate him from Alden but also to encourage his abilities. And I felt the program was going to be a good fit for our kid.

All weekend I pondered the incident at Mapleton Montessori and decided to ask my colleagues at the gifted kids support network if they had encountered that behavior before.

On Monday, I called Carol and another colleague, Mary. Mary had an immediate suggestion. "Donna, you should get Julian an occupational therapy evaluation. I've seen kids get so much calmer with OT. He may have some sensory integration issues. I have a referral name for you."

I was thankful for her input and decided to set up an evaluation for the following week. In the meantime, I was off in a new direction, learning all about occupational therapy and sensory integration disorder. It was a new chapter in working with giftedness. In the process, I found that Julian definitely needed occupational therapy, and that led me to weekly OT sessions during which he learned to manage the plethora of sensory input he received in his body and mind. His overwhelm in the playground had been caused by the large number of kids playing loudly around him, and that overstimulation caused him to panic and climb the fence.

Understanding this about my son helped me be a better advocate for him in finding the next school and teachers. We decided to start Julian in first grade a year late so he could have another year of kindergarten, adding OT and more time with the supportive teachers at Mapleton Montessori.

But as I found more balance for myself, moved ahead with my career, and felt stronger as a mom, I felt I was never quite managing as a wife. I was always struggling with how to find a better flow with Peter and Julian as a family. And I felt I was definitely having to carry the burden of making all the parenting decisions and managing the day-to-day issues we were encountering.

More and more, I sought out other moms for support and scheduled playdates away from home to create more community and fun for Julian and me. I sought something outside my family that wasn't happening inside it, and I didn't know how to make it better.

Chapter Three

Divorce When You Don't See It Coming

EVEN IF THE SIGNS that major change is coming are there, we don't always see them when our focus is on just managing our everyday lives. And I had plenty to manage in my everyday life. As Julian started first grade in our neighborhood public school, Peter and I both hoped we were going to settle into something more normalized with our kid. Peter coached him in soccer, I took him to Suzuki violin lessons, and we both hoped for the best.

Julian's second grade year brought more challenges and more problem-solving, which strained our relationship again. Over time, Peter seemed to develop a distaste for both the marriage and joint parenting, and I found his behavior confusing. I'd thought he was excited about Julian's giftedness, but in second grade, Julian had also been diagnosed with attention deficit hyperactivity disorder (ADHD), and Peter seemed to have difficulty handling the challenges that accompanied it. Julian was in public school, and he needed an individual education plan to succeed there. On the one hand, the ADHD diagnosis helped with that, but on the other hand, there was a stigma attached to that diagnosis.

The greater challenge for me during Julian's second grade school year was helping him manage his activity level so he could settle down and focus while not shutting him down when he was excited. I learned over the next few years that these were the traits of a "twice-exceptional" child, which meant that he had both gifted traits and learning disabilities. His main gifted trait, his creativity, was hard to recognize because of his processing and nonverbal learning disabilities. Those challenges made it difficult for him to settle down and pay attention when he was bored or disinterested. Sorting all of this out wasn't easy, and my deep study of giftedness generated questions. Did Julian need to be medicated? How could we control his learning environment so he could be successful enough to progress without emotional disturbance?

Questions like those sometimes led to disagreements between Peter and me, and I didn't understand how to work with our conflicts. When Peter disagreed with me over meds or how to handle Julian's behaviors, he simply shut down. We were unable to talk things through to a resolution. This was hard for me because I wanted to process things verbally. I'd make sure Peter came with us to doctor's appointments, and he'd engage with the doctor, but then we would not talk about things afterward. I wanted to take the traditional route, work with the school system, and put Julian on meds temporarily so he could feel successful. But Peter didn't want him on meds, even when the doctors told us it was the right step. We were not working together. I chose to move forward with what I felt was the right next step for Julian without Peter's involvement. And as Julian moved into third grade, he was slowly getting better at school in reading and math while on Adderall.

I finally realized that Peter was talking with his mother about family issues without including me. She lived outside Seattle, Washington, and only saw us on holidays and vacations she arranged to see us. My having taken Julian to Florida the day she arrived to see him right after his birth hadn't helped, but we'd worked to rebuild our relationship. I could see some similarities between Peter and his mother when it came to handling emotional issues and considered the possibility that he might be turning to her for advice to get his own support.

We were vacationing at Kauai in her timeshare condominium in June of 1999 when Peter showed me his true feelings. We had just tried to make love in our bedroom, but he turned away and walked over to the window. "What's going on with you?" I asked. "You seem really disinterested and distant."

"I'm done," he replied before sighing and turning to look at me earnestly. His eyes were dark and full of something I wasn't sure I recognized but might have been sorrow. "I don't love you anymore, and I'm done. I want a divorce." There was no warmth in his words, just cold precision.

The words stuck in the air. It was as if I were in a snowstorm and couldn't see him across the room. Shock and disbelief froze my body, and I had to leave the room. I left the condo and went outside to the walkway that led to the plush grass and palm trees nearby. It was a spot I had visited many times during the two weeks of our vacation there. It was comforting and warm, and I felt the trees holding me in my despair.

Peter followed me out there, and that made me really mad. "Why are you following me? You just told me you didn't want to be with me anymore. Leave me alone."

I turned to walk farther away from him, but he came over to me and grabbed my hand. A part of me was relieved by that thread of connection. I broke through my trance and looked at his face. His eyes were as cold and precise as his words had been. I knew it was over with that look, regardless of anything I might say or do. "What did I do?" I asked. "I know that's a stupid question to ask at this point, but I have to ask."

"It's not worth going into it, Donna. I just can't do this anymore."

He let go of my hand, and I walked as far from him as I could get on that grassy lawn and still be able to talk to him as I looked out into the Pacific Ocean to calm myself. But as I spoke, anger crept into my voice. "So we're on vacation with your parents and our kid. How do you propose we go through the next day and the trip home?"

"We just act normal, and we'll deal with this when we get home. We don't want to make a scene with my mom and Dick."

So that's what we did. We just stuffed the vomit all back in and acted like we were in perfect health in our family. It was all about saving face for Peter and presenting the right message for his folks. I gave it a good try, but it was hard to hide my anger and sadness because inside, I was seething. Still, I didn't want to make a scene that would upset Julian's vacation with his grandparents.

When we got home, it was icy cold between us. There wasn't enough warmth for us to talk further or even provide the space for my feelings. It seemed like the same feeling I sometimes had when I was with my family in Florida. He was out the door and headed to an attorney's office. And Julian felt it big time. I couldn't hide my upset any more than Julian could, though I tried to be strong around him, and I fell apart when I was with my friends and colleagues.

I immediately got Julian a child and family therapist and went into therapy myself. I was distraught and in shock. Then I reluctantly looked for an attorney, though I didn't want to do it that way at all. I hoped we could talk things through and do some mediation. Peter's mom was an attorney, and he had probably been advised by her to get an attorney pronto. I felt betrayed and maneuvered.

Somehow, we managed to get through that first year. Peter moved out immediately and bought his own place. I got a renter for the basement and stayed in the big house on Sixth Street, our home since Julian was one. The renter was a temporary nanny for Julian, and that helped give me additional child care so I could continue my practice. We moved into a temporary visitation schedule with Peter having Mondays and Tuesdays and me having Wednesdays through Fridays and every other weekend.

That schedule began to cause issues for Julian at school. His fourth grade teacher, Mr. Maron, called me in one day to observe. "Julian is struggling, today especially. It seems this happens every time he is at his dad's house."

"Is he acting like he's on his meds or not?" I asked, wondering if Peter was giving him his Adderall. Peter had been dead set against meds from the start, so that was definitely a possibility.

"He can't seem to settle down and focus, and he seems disconnected from me and the other kids. He's much better later in the week when he's at your house."

Mr. Maron had immediately connected with Julian when school started. Mr. Maron had ADHD or some kind of learning disability in his past, which he revealed to me at our first meeting for Julian's individual education plan, so they had something in common. Considering how connected he was to Julian, the fact that he was concerned about him was upsetting to me. If Peter wasn't giving Julian his meds, how could I do anything about it? I began to worry deeply and felt anger bubbling up.

"Let's just observe him and take some notes," I suggested, remembering that getting into more conflict would only hurt Julian and create more struggles for him at school. The most important thing was to help Julian stay successful in his school-work. That helped him socially and emotionally. Over and over, I had been told that by medical professionals.

"Do you think you could check with his dad about the meds?" Mr. Maron asked.

"I wouldn't touch that with a ten-foot pole," I replied. "I fear that will just cause more stress for Julian."

Mr. Moran furrowed his brow. "Let's see. Maybe you could hang out a while and observe a bit more."

I was feeling exasperated. "I'm afraid Julian will get self-conscious and worried that I'm here. I think it's better that you support him in the ways you know best, Mr. Moran. You're his favorite teacher."

I left the classroom and headed home on foot, feeling the worry and anger coming to the surface as I walked. Fortunately, I'd walked the six blocks from home, which gave me a chance to let off some steam on the way back. If Peter was not giving Julian his meds, it was total sabotage for our kid. And the only way to talk about it was to have Peter speak with Mr. Moran, which would keep me from being in the middle. I decided to ask Mr. Moran to set up a conference with Peter.

I needed to step back and let Peter step up to the plate.

A year later, it was clear to me I had to sell the Sixth Street house and move Julian to a smaller home. The cost of a nanny, mortgage, and other expenses necessitated the move. I had found a small bungalow that would work for the time being, and it was close to Julian's school and Peter's new home. But selling the huge house and property was a burden on me.

I was officially divorced, and Julian was adjusting better to the parenting schedule, but he was not doing much better at school. In fact, he had a very inexperienced fifth grade teacher, and she was unable to handle his behavior in a supportive way. She had shamed him, and he started acting like the class clown. I was very upset about that, but the principal refused my requests to move him to the other fifth grade classroom. My only way of coping was to keep Julian in therapy.

I did manage to sell the house, and on moving day, I found memories of our nine years there flowing out of me as I cried tears of anger, sadness, and regret. The tears were followed by fear. How would I manage to move into and set up my new house in the state I was in? How would I manage my life with Julian on my own? It all felt scary. I didn't want to raise my kid on my own, and I'd never wanted the divorce. I was angry. Why had Peter left me to sell the house, pack up, and clean up the mess? It was his damned mess! I wasn't ready to face my fear of being alone, so I was holding onto fear and anger.

My neighbor and friend, Carla, came by and was my sounding board as we sorted things and cleaned up the garage. The familiar rush of anger swelled up inside me, and she just listened and kept nudging me on. I noticed that I was able to keep my anger in check a little after the initial outburst and realized that it was because my friend was there, loving me as I let it all out.

I felt held enough to hold myself a bit. *What a concept*, I thought. *I'm letting her love in.* I continued to move through the cleaning tasks with a bit more lightness.

She guided me in sweeping and doing the final touches on the garage, filling my car with as much as it could hold, and building a throwaway pile nearby. And then we walked back into the house. I noticed how different it felt being back in the house with her there with me. I could breathe better, and I settled myself into a chair while she moved to the stove and made me some tea. I felt nurtured by her care of me. She'd been through divorce too and had learned how strong she was from it. I wasn't feeling all that strong, but I appreciated having someone who knew what I was going through with me.

The following day, Peter was coming over to take down the tree house, and having some support before facing that was good. Just the thought of the tree house triggered a flood of memories. Peter had designed and built the three-level tree house in our favorite catalpa tree, and he had even included a drawbridge. It was an enchanting structure, and from its third level, we could see Mount Sanitas and scan the whole north Boulder foothills.

In that vulnerable state, I dropped into the memory of an idyllic day when Julian was in second grade, before he started feeling bad about his issues. We walked home from his school and spent the whole afternoon together up in the tree house.

"I want to lower the drawbridge for you, Mom," he'd yelled to me as he ran to the drawbridge and moved the pulley to lower it into a flat plank so I could walk into his playhouse from the ground level, which was where I liked to enter it. I ducked my head and stepped onto the drawbridge with my backpack of books and snacks. As I walked into the first level, he closed the drawbridge behind me.

He seemed so proud of himself as he swung up the outside of the little castle to the second level, which was the way he liked to enter it, and then dropped the ladder that allowed me to climb up to the next level, where he was waiting for me smiling like a happy knight welcoming me into his castle.

"I see you climbing like a monkey, making this amazing machinery in your castle work. Are you the master knight of this castle?" I asked, knowing he loved playing with costumes and being a knight in his tree house castle.

As I warmed myself with the memory of that day, I remembered what had been in the background that afternoon. I'd been worrying about the school meeting I had just attended during which I'd been told that Julian needed to be tested for ADHD. I'd been upset by the conversation because I had tried everything up to that point to avoid that diagnosis. When he was in preschool, I'd been told that occupational therapy would help him with his some of his asynchronous development (a symptom of gifted kids) and would prevent him from being diagnosed with ADHD. He had completed two years of occupational therapy by then, and I'd thought he just had learning disabilities and was learning ways to overcome them.

That day, I climbed to the upper level of the tree house, which was open with no sides, except for a railing. Julian was already waiting there for me, and I was ready to sit, read, and eat some snacks. But just as I settled into a cross-legged position, Julian jumped up.

"I'm heading to the crow's nest, Mom," he'd announced as he headed up to the swinging rope ladder that connected the level we'd been on together with a much smaller basket-shaped landing up in the bigger branches of the tree. There was only room for one in the crow's nest, but just like a ship's crow's nest, it was a great lookout spot. Julian had been enchanted by the sailing stories Peter had told him, which was how he'd learned about ship crow's nests, and then Peter built him a crow's nest.

I was a bit frightened of the spot because of its height, and I'd never been able to get over my fear to climb up all the way into it. But I was learning about my son and trying to accept that he thrived on that kind of adventure and activity.

I asked if he wanted some snacks before he went up there, but he was already gone. He'd needed to blow off steam, and the tree house had really helped him with that after school. He just wanted to play a while and said that he never got enough time to just hang out in the tree house with me. I did hang out with him there. It had actually helped me as well as him, allowing me to be a bit more active before we had to go in for homework and dinner prep. What was unspoken was that his father, who had built the tree house, rarely hung out with him there.

When he asked why I'd been talking to his teachers that day, I told him that we were trying to get him more time with Cecily, the reading aide, so he could catch up in reading with the other kids in class.

"Whatever!" he'd replied. "I'd rather read here than at school. What book are we reading today?" He was soon down from the crow's nest and reading. He got stuck on some letters, but he'd come a long way.

When I came out of my reverie, I looked up at Carla.

"Honey, you look like you are in so much pain," she said. "What are you thinking?"

"I guess I'm struggling with how to go on from here. It all feels overwhelming!"

She nodded. "Of course it does. It's normal to feel over-whelmed with a divorce that totally changes everything. I've been through it myself, and I know how hard it is. Nathan has had lots of behavior issues since his dad and I split, and he prob-ably has ADHD, but we haven't wanted to get him tested. I've moved him to the Waldorf School, and he's better. It does slow-ly settle down. You'll sort it all out in time. I promise you."

I hated that I was moving away from her and the neighbor-hood, but I wasn't going too far.

She was tracking my expression, and without saying a word, she walked over and gave me a hug again. I could hardly feel her body against mine, but I greatly appreciated her being there. Someday I would feel again, but it was hard right then to deal with so much emotion coming and going with everything. It felt overwhelming and numbing.

Carla got up and started toward the door. "Donna, my dear, you know where I am if you need to talk or cry or anything else. I want to get back home for Nathan."

I nodded and wordlessly, emotionally, walked her to the door, let her out, and closed it behind her. Then I sat down, and the tears flowed.

I moved into my new house, and as the days went by, I kept asking myself why I was so angry. Why couldn't I get over the divorce? Neither my anger nor my inability to get over the divorce could be understood fully in any cursory way. Like many things human, there was complexity to both, and that complexity took time to unravel.

It took years of learning to listen to my anger in my trauma therapy and meditation classes before I began to understand why my anger was so big. And its origin predated my relationship with Peter. I learned that from the time I was a newborn infant, crying with colic and unable to be calmed, my mother had been repelled by my discomfort. She hadn't known how to console me. I felt her discomfort, so I got more and more angry and raged to try to get some connection. But my anger created more disconnection. Soon I learned how to shut down my intensity so I could get the loving attention I craved.

That began the process of programming myself to shut down my anger and other big feelings. It created a difficult cycle of anxious attachment, causing me to distrust my mother early on, and later, causing me to distrust friends and partners in relationships. Anger told me something wasn't right, and I needed to learn to listen so I could find what was better for me.

But long before I fully understood the origin of my relationship with anger, I began to learn how to work with my intense feelings. In fits and starts, and with the help of my therapist, I was able to slow down my overwhelming feelings over the next year or so. I had to be guided in therapy to come to the present moment, experience my feelings in my body, and stop rushing to understand my emotions in my head. It was training in learning to notice and accept what was happening in the present moment. That was what being mindful was all about, but I didn't know that yet.

Finally I got some clarity from it all. First, I realized I felt betrayed. I had worked hard to survive in what the marriage had become, and I'd never given a thought to giving up like he had. For me, marriage was a commitment for life, and I'd seen that modeled in my parents' lifelong commitment to our family. Peter's parents, both single children, had masked their marital conflicts and had left Peter alone a lot. They'd separated after he left at eighteen.

I had grown up in a family of seven children with much connection, activity, and overt conflict. Hell, my parents had arguments at the dinner table in front of all seven of us. It was rather traumatizing, but it certainly brought me face-to-face with their marital power conflict. Because of that, I was willing to work through conflicts and go into therapy instead of staying stuck like they had been. I was hoping Peter would figure out what he needed and that our love would carry us through. I never let myself think about divorce.

But the real reason the divorce was so devastating to me emotionally was that I couldn't accept it. I couldn't reconcile the part of me that was so convinced that the marriage was right for me with the part of me that understood it was over. Had I made a major mistake by marrying Peter? Did I not know what was best for me? How could I deal with the self-criticism and self-blaming that made my pain even worse? I was fighting myself inside. I couldn't begin to turn the page of my life story because I was still holding onto the dream of the adventurous life I had created for myself in Colorado with Peter. That life had helped me find myself so powerfully. I strongly believed it had been the best thing I'd ever done in my life up to that point.

I'd forgotten that my own personal dream to find adventure in Colorado had actually brought me to the state.

I had been drawn to Colorado ever since my maternal great-aunt, Margaret (known as Bob), had told me stories about riding horses across the Continental Divide from Denver to Steamboat Springs with her friends, Eleanor Bliss and Marjorie Perry, in the 1920s. My aunt had been one of my strongest role models growing up, and even though she was living in Florida in the 1970s, she and Eleanor Bliss—who continued to live in Colorado—were still correspondents. Aunt Bob paved the way for my move to Colorado in 1976 by writing to Eleanor, who became a huge resource for me when I was putting down roots in Steamboat Springs. On my arrival that summer, Eleanor gave me a place to stay, let me ride her horse, and introduced me to some of Steamboat's best people. Seeing and being with an independent woman who loved adventure like Eleanor gave me the ability to see that I could also become a strong woman. And I had. I had been living that dream in Colorado, and the divorce didn't need to end it.

That realization was powerful. Growing up in Florida, I had been taught to do the "right" thing, which was neither about freedom or adventure. But when I moved to Colorado, I discovered a freer and more playful way of being. Peter had been the main opening for my connection with the outdoors, but moving on in my life apart from him was about reconnecting with who I was becoming as a strong woman, an athlete, and a mother.

The adventurer, the aspect of myself that loved being adventurous in nature, was expanding me into a deeper understanding of who I was as a woman and how to be more present and alive inside. It awakened my curiosity for deeper self-discovery. Nature and outdoor adventures in Colorado were a strong portal into myself, leading me to feeling my strengths and other expansive parts of me that I hadn't explored much growing up.

Chapter Four

Single Mom

JULIAN AND I SETTLED INTO a remodeled 1952 bungalow on a major street in the same neighborhood, just a few blocks from Peter's new home with his new wife, Patty. We were close enough that Julian could walk between our homes in keeping with his visitation schedule. I was hoping that things would get back to something like normal, but my life had drastically changed, and there was a new normal.

My body was showing me that the current stress of that new normal was having an impact. At fifty-one, the previous two years of divorce stress had kicked me into menopause with symptoms that disturbed my daily routine a lot. Night sweats awakened me at two in the morning daily, and even though I turned on newly installed bedroom fans to blast me, I was unable to get back to sleep successfully for very long. I was running on four or five hours of sleep and trying to find natural remedies to help me cope. The sleeping issues reminded me of my postpartum depression and how shifting hormones and stress impacted my ability to sleep. I was feeling anxiety and panic again, and my greatest fear was that I would become depressed.

I felt depleted and battered, but I realized I had to get my shit together—and fast. I had a kid to raise and a private practice to grow. How was I going to get myself calmed down and functional? I tried to dig deeper into myself to figure out my priorities.

First and foremost, I really wanted to be a good mom to Julian. I didn't feel I was doing a very good job at the moment. I was getting too wound up in reactions and feelings about everything, which meant that I couldn't be calm and present enough to be consistent with my parenting. Everything I was hearing and learning about twice-exceptional kids was that they needed consistency and rhythm in their day. I had to work on myself more to be the parent that Julian needed.

Second, I wanted a relationship that worked. To find a healthier relationship for me, which included someone who could help me create a new and more functional family life for Julian, I needed to work on myself. But I was confused about what would be a healthy relationship for me. Everything I had done with Peter felt right until it wasn't. I thought the problem was that I got too emotional and overwhelmed and couldn't work through those feelings very well, so I started exploring how to be *with* my feelings more, which I thought might help me understand what happened when I got intense or overwhelmed. I had ignored my intensity in the past, and now it was time to befriend myself.

To do that, I needed to learn how to slow down more and observe myself. While I had made inroads on changing my pattern of pushing myself physically to get through everything, I had not completely overcome that pattern. But I couldn't push myself as I had in the past because menopause was speaking to me, and it was completely reconfiguring my body systems. I could either make it a challenge or I could make it a transformative experience. I chose the latter, so I read everything I could about menopause. I learned that it was a time of personal reckoning. Dr. Christiane Northrup's book, *The Wisdom of Menopause*, emphasized the importance of midlife for women and how we needed to stay healthy physically, psychologically, and spiritually so we could bring our wisdom forward. Because most of us had been taking care of others until then, our bodies were designed to bring forth our greatest contributions in our post-menopausal years.

When I reread her chapter on emotional health, in which she talked about old wounding coming to the surface to be healed at menopause, I really understood what she was saying. My body was showing me that it was time to slow down, go within, and listen. Unresolved grief and pain needed to be addressed or it would shut your body down through things like depression, physical illnesses, and autoimmune diseases. That really got my attention, and I wondered about how to resolve my grief and pain.

So the third and biggest impetus to do more inner work was to get clarity and wisdom about where and how to go forward in my life to heal and to harvest my feminine wisdom. I felt that coming forth, and I wanted to open up to it, but I was too tired and too worn out. I would learn that there were other aspects or "parts" of myself that needed to be known and freed up inside me to allow my wholeness and wisdom to fully blossom.

I discovered that I could embrace Northrup's words when I started to slow down and notice what my body was showing me instead of listening to my mind, which was trying to figure it all out. I began exploring yoga as a way to learn from my body. Bikram Yoga was one way I learned how to focus on my body and my breath and to get present. Somehow, when I left a yoga class, I felt that all the internal debris had been blown out, and I was calm and open instead of angry and anxious.

✧ ✧ ✧

"Now move into Tree Pose, keeping your breath steady," the instructor rang out loudly. "Thirty seconds holding it here."

I stood there sweating from head to toe as I pulled my right foot across my left knee, squeezing my muscles tighter on my left quad to hold the pose and lifting my body taller so I could balance as I reached out and completed the pose by holding my right toe with my left hand. Ooh, I could feel my right hip yelp at me. I knew to just breathe into the struggle because it would-n't be for very long.

"Change. Good," the instructor said. "Now, finish off this standing series with Toe Stand, or Padangustasana. Important for strengthening feet, this pose expands range of motion in the ankles, knees, and hips. It also requires and builds mental stam-ina and focus."

I always struggled with Toe Stand, so I just did my best to stay balanced as people around me went down farther than I could. I kept telling myself that however I did it that day, it was okay. I was glad we were done with the standing series, and I was looking forward to the resting between poses we did on the floor poses.

"Change. Now find your way to your mat for our short rest in Savasana before we move into the floor series."

I collapsed onto the mat that was already drenched, but my towel was over it so it wasn't too wet. Then I closed my eyes and squeezed my shoulders to release the tension between my neck and back. I pressed my back and shoulders into the mat to get that grounded feeling I loved as I stretched out my legs, letting my toes tip out, and placed my hands faceup at my sides.

"Keep your eyes open and just focus on your breathing. Stay right here in this room and notice your body and your breath."

I opened my eyes and tried to get present. All I felt was my sweating body, but it was a good feeling because so much of it felt released and opened already.

After what felt like five minutes, he said, "Change. Moving into Wind Removing Pose, bend your right knee up to your shoulder and extend your left leg on the mat, toes up and flexed foot. Now bring your arms down on your shin, pulling it closer—as close as you can to your body. This pose clears your large intestine and releases any toxins there"

My focus drifted off until I heard, "Bring your hands over your head to prepare for your first Sit-Up, exhaling once now and then again as you sit up straight and reach your feet. Turn around and lie on your belly to start Cobra Pose."

I must have done the double leg wind removing pose unconsciously, somehow disassociated, I thought. Feeling connected again, I noticed how much I loved the spine strengthening series on the floor because I got to practice resting in between each pose since we did each pose twice. I curled my spine up, leading with the back of my head and pushing off with my palms at my sides. That was good. Then we placed our right ear on the mat and stretched our necks. And then we did Cobra again and the left ear on the mat. I loved the breathing and stopping. It felt like just what my body wanted, and I noticed tightness draining out of my neck.

"Ready for your second Sit-Up. Ready. Exhale."

I had dropped off with my focus, enjoying relaxing my neck and body, but I rolled over and did my Sit-Up pose, trying to catch up with the class.

"Now back on your belly. Prepare for Locust Pose, placing both hands palm-down under your belly or as far as you can to give you the support you will need for this pose."

I was already into the pose, lifting my right leg and then my left. Then I readjusted my arms, bringing them together under my belly, and lifted both legs. It was a hard pose. I let my legs fall down to the mat and reluctantly followed the instructions to roll over on my back and do a Sit-Up again and then go back down to do Locust again. I told myself I didn't want to do it again, and I had to keep my body moving through the difficult lift. The rest of the class was easy from there, so I let go more.

Somehow, we were at the final twist when I was suddenly present again for the pose and the Kapalabhati breathing that ended the class. I dropped into the final Savasana and closed my eyes, noticing a huge settling in my mind. It felt so good, I totally let go.

I woke up five minutes later and noticed that everyone had left the space except me and another woman I couldn't see because she was behind me but whose voice was familiar when I heard her speak my name. I decided to drag myself up and roll up my mat. It was Sheila, my former dentist, and I wondered why I hadn't seen her before. She noticed me too, so I walked over, gave her a big hug, and walked out into the hall where we could talk.

"How are you?" I asked as I looked into her sweaty face. "I'm a mess right now, but it's good to see you." I pulled at my wet, sweaty hair, trying to put it in place.

"I'm just okay, Donna," she said, looking off in the distance instead of at me. "You know, I'm going through a divorce." Then she looked back at me. "I heard through the grapevine you were too. I'm so sorry, Donna."

"Yes, it's true. Our boys will have lots to talk about when they grow up, huh?" -

She said she had to go and seemed in a hurry to leave, so that was the end of our conversation.

As I walked to the dressing room to shower and put on my work clothes, my thoughts went to our friendship when our sons had been together at Mapleton Montessori years earlier. I had lost track of their family since we'd stopped going to her as a dentist. She was a professional just like me, and I had always respected her as a woman. She was bright and fun.

Seeing Sheila at Bikram was comforting. I wasn't alone. Other professional women had divorces too, and it was a huge disruption for their kids and families too. I felt less shame when I saw her.

Kana was another professional mother who had been through divorce. She was a Realtor and the mom of two boys. The youngest, Quinn, had befriended Julian in their class at Foothills Elementary School. Kana was different from the other moms I had befriended over the past few years. She was in the middle of what I was beginning to face myself. She was juggling kids, school issues, and troubles with her ex while trying to keep herself above the negativity. It was powerful to see her determination and strength.

She had remarried and was transitioning into a new life with a new husband, so her life was moving forward. That she had turned a life corner was exciting to me because I felt stuck. When Quinn invited Julian over for a play date, not only did Quinn and Julian begin a wonderful and supportive relationship, so did Kana and I.

Kana was finding some peace in her new life, but there were still many co-parenting issues with her ex, who continued to see Quinn and his brother every week. Her older son had some school issues that caused co-parenting friction and conflict similar to Julian's. Quinn, on the other hand, a strong student and athlete, was weathering the divorce well. Julian's self-esteem grew through his relationship with Quinn, as well as through sports, music, and scouting activities. Kana and her family began to feel like extended family to us.

As Julian was moving toward middle school, I thought about what school might be best for him and wanted to consider one

across town as an option. But that would require regular carpool-
ing, and Peter was not interested in that plan. I decided to talk
with Kana about it and explained the situation to her one day at
her home.

"Peter won't support my decision to send Julian across town
to middle school. I think the best school for him is Manhattan.
It's across town, and we would have to carpool. He's so negative
about all my decisions, and he won't talk about anything with
me. I'm trying to find the right school for Julian's needs. It's so
difficult working with Peter as a co-parent. I hate it. I wish I had
more of the decision-making."

"I get it," she replied. "I had the same struggles when I was
trying to get Shaun's school situation working better. I had him
on meds, and he was so angry about the divorce. He was ten
when it happened, just like Julian. It all got better when I found
a great therapist who was able to work with my ex and me and
do some family work. It saved us."

"Really? I would love to find a family therapist who could
help us. What made it better for you? How did it help Shaun?"

"I got the support I needed as a divorced mom from Len. He
helped me see how to be stronger and more consistent with
Shaun, even though I felt guilty about his struggles. And he has
a son about Shaun's age with similar challenges. He bonded
with Shaun well, and he helped Shaun develop the self-esteem
to move on in his life."

The therapist's name was Len McPherson, and he not only
worked individually with Shaun, he also did family therapy
work that included Kana's ex-husband. It sounded like the family had really benefited from working with Len.-

"Okay, that solves one problem. I'll call him. The other
problem is, I don't have a nanny who can drive. I can't do the
carpools every morning and afternoon, and even if we can get

a neighborhood carpool together, I still can't do afternoons. I'm at a loss as to how to make this work, even if he gets accepted at Manhattan."

Kana had a brilliant suggestion. "Donna, let me be your next nanny. I have had to cut back on my hours, and Millard isn't making enough right now, so we could use a little regular income. We would be supporting each other. What do you think?"

I admitted it was a great idea and told her I'd think about it. I wanted to be sure that having Julian around all the time would be okay for her and her boys, and I needed to check with Julian before making a final decision. My heart was ready to go, but it also needed to be worked through in my head. On the way home with Julian, we talked it through. He was excited about hanging out at their house. My biggest concern was getting his homework done, which would be my next conversation with Kana.

But I wasn't just relieved about the possibility of having the nanny situation worked out. It was more than that. I felt heard and cared for by Kana, and it had felt good to verbally process things with her. It had helped me slow down and feel my feelings in the moment.

I flashed on difficult situations when I was growing up and my mom sat me down to talk about what I was feeling. Maybe she saw me as intense or confused and was determined to fix whatever it was that was bothering me. But however she saw it, she tried to tell me what I was feeling instead of asking me and letting me unpack it myself. So I believed I couldn't understand my feelings myself. That belief had never served me.

But Kana had been open to hearing my feelings just as they came out, and she had been so loving that I could bring that love into myself more and listen more deeply within. It was healing for me to be held by her in that way, and I thought my openness helped her too. I realized I needed that loving attention to help me find myself again and feel supported enough to explore my intensity more.

Kana and I developed a plan that worked. She picked up the boys in the afternoon, and they had both regular playtime and regular homework time before I picked up Julian. Often, we met at a restaurant not far from my office and had dinner together before Julian and I left for home. It was like having a supportive co-parent and a girlfriend all in one person.

As I searched for support from other parents, we joined a local United Church of Christ church, and I began teaching Sunday School for Julian's class of twenty-four kids. My help was greatly appreciated, and it felt good to serve in that way. Going back to a Christian Church was familiar to me, and it was a great support. Growing up, my sensitivity and spiritedness had been seen as strong faith and curiosity at my church.

I also signed up to be a Webelos Scouts leader and organized Julian's scout program with another mom for that year. As I worked with other boys his age in that scout group, I saw kids with learning issues and ADD, and I was able to share some of my struggles and get support as well as return support to other parents. That give-and-take was freeing, and I felt less isolated in my parenting struggles. I also had the opportunity to go with scouts and their families on weekend camping trips. Not only did that give me more time to be in nature with Julian and an opportunity to develop deeper relationships with several of the parents, it gave me the much-needed grounding I felt in nature.

It was validation that I needed to be in nature as much as possible to balance out the stresses of work and co-parenting and express my intensity. I needed moorings as a single mom, and I was grateful for that one.

Chapter Five

New Ways of Being

I TOOK KANA'S RECOMMENDATION of Len as therapist and started Julian with regular sessions of play therapy and then family therapy with me. I'd wanted Peter to be a part of the family therapy sessions too, but he declined.

One afternoon that fall, Len called me into his office from the waiting room after he had completed his session with Julian. "Julian just did the most disturbing thing in his play, Donna. He acted out a scene in the dollhouse where everyone was knocking down the doors and walls and hitting each other. I have never seen him act out such anger and rage. There's something he's trying to tell me, Donna." Instead of sitting down at his desk, he walked across his office away from me as he talked and then turned around as I responded.

"Oh, my God! I can't believe this. I've never seen any anger like that." I looked up at Len with a grimace. "What should we do?" I was already down the road, trying to solve the problem—my usual pattern.

"Knowing Julian, he's letting me know it's all getting to him. He's been in enough therapy, and this is the ultimate display of his frustration. He's really angry, and we need to find out why."

"Did he say this?"

"No, he acted it all out. He just needed to release it, and that was therapeutic. But something is really working on him, and we need to be curious about what it is." He finally sat down in his chair in front of me. He often sat at his desk with his chair turned toward me as I sat on the sofa, but that day he leaned out with his hands toward me as if to cue me to work harder on the problem.

I stood up and paced while talking. "Well, his dad isn't hitting him. I can tell you that. It might be the going back-and-forth that is really the problem. I'm wondering if I'm not giving him permission to share his feelings in some way. He doesn't have the ability to tell his dad how it feels, so I should get more of his feelings. Maybe he's feeling pressured and can't talk about it." My brain was going a mile a minute, trying to figure it out, and I was getting more upset by the moment.

Len came over and put his hand on my shoulder. "It's going to be okay, Donna. We'll figure this out."

I finally sat back down.

"Let's bring him in and see what he wants to tell you," he suggested.

This was standard family therapy procedure, but I wasn't liking that Len hadn't gotten any answers when he was alone with Julian. When Julian came in, he was shut down, and I could see there wasn't going to be anything productive from him at that point. I had seen that behavior before, and it was troubling to me.

The session was soon over, and Julian and I went home. When I got home and Julian was playing outside, I called Len back. I felt anger flaring up and realized the situation with Julian was just another trigger for me. I was doing everything I could do to help my son, and yet, it was possible that the ways I was trying to help him through the divorce was making him worse. I had to figure out what to do next.

Len answered the phone on the first ring. "Len, I have a follow-up question about today's session. Should I get an attorney and push for full decision-making? Right now we share educational and medical decision-making, and it isn't working well. Peter doesn't talk to me about what's happening at his house— or anything else. We have no communication. This has to be impacting Julian. Can you call him again and ask him to come in?"

"Donna, you definitely ought to have that control," Len replied. You're so clear about what's right for Julian. You're such a good mom."

His words made me speechless. Until he'd said them, I hadn't realized I needed to hear them. I let the validation enter me slowly. I realized that I'd been going to therapist after therapist for the past three years because I wasn't feeling good about my parenting. But why? I considered the fact that Peter had never said anything positive about me as a mom. In fact, I'd had to fight his negative attitude, indifference, and lack of support and just push through by myself. I kept blaming myself for all the problems and Julian's challenges as my way of coping. It was my habitual way of reacting when something went wrong. I hadn't been able to see it before, but now I was coming to my senses and hearing the validation I needed to move on.

Len said he would reach out to Peter again, but he didn't think anything would change there. He suggested we do some mediation to change the parenting schedule so I had more control to make decisions for Julian rather than go through attorneys again. I had been through two attorneys at that point and did not want to have anything more to do with them.

Before I could take a step, Peter's attorney sent out an Order for Modification of Parenting Plan, proposing a switch to a fifty-fifty parenting schedule. I knew it was about money and not about wanting to parent Julian more, and I knew I would need an attorney to counter the request because he wouldn't talk to me about it. I also knew that attorneys usually recommended a parental responsibility evaluation (PRE) in situations like this. A PRE was like being under the microscope as a parent, and the idea of it fueled my rage and took me right over the edge. The process felt demeaning and unnecessary, and it made me feel like a bad parent. I didn't want to be like all those other divorced parents who couldn't talk about how to best meet the needs of their child.

Mostly I was angry because of the impact this would have on Julian. When parents were unable to talk to each other, the kids ended up having to manage their own feelings and needs, and it was very stressful for them. It affected their social and emotional health and their performance in school and other activities. Parental responsibility evaluations could prolong the family conflict and traumatize the kids more. Sometimes they were helpful if parents were totally in conflict, but they took the decisions away from the parents and put them into the hands of mental health professionals and attorneys. Was that really where my family was at? I couldn't believe it.

I met with Len again, and we agreed it was best to push for mediation instead of the PRE. I hired an attorney I liked who had been recommended by Len, but we ended up having to complete the parental responsibility evaluation anyway. It was a very emotionally difficult two months, and the recommendations got us nowhere. Peter and his attorney recommended we throw out the whole evaluation. My attorney proposed mediation with Len, and fortunately, they agreed to it. We were able to get most of the parental decisions turned over to me as the custodial parent, and that ended the main co-parenting conflicts.

Even though all divorcing parents in Colorado were required to take a co-parenting class, many parents continued to behave in harmful ways with their children, who were already coping with conflicts between their parents and the stress of navigating going back-and-forth between two homes. I was imagining several ways Julian might be getting unhealthy messages at his dad's house that were causing him distress. And I realized that *my* anger might not be giving him room to experience *his own* anger at home with me. I hoped I could change that by focusing more on my parenting and slowing myself down.

Over time and after the change in the visitation schedule and parental decision-making was in place, Julian began to feel more comfortable and settled in my home since he was only visiting his dad and Patty every other weekend.

I was still worried about the impact of all this on Julian when he did something amazing. In sixth grade, he was enrolled in the special education program so he could get an individual learning plan (IEP). But he had all of his classes in the mainstream classrooms except for a special ed study hall. He hated being in a classroom designated "special ed" for a whole period, even though it was only a supported study hall. In response to how that made him feel, he told his special ed teacher he was not ADHD and no longer needed to take his meds.

After talking through that decision with him, I knew he wanted to be "normal" like the other kids. It was clear he was deciding that for himself. Somehow, he was empowered by his dad's position on the meds. I learned a lot from my son on that day. He was taking charge and no longer being victimized by his learning disabilities. He was charting his own course, and I decided to support him going forward, in spite of my fears.

I was told kids like him could learn to compensate with the right teaching in the right settings. So with my new control of educational and medical decisions, I was able to move ahead with my plan for getting Julian into a private school for seventh and eighth grades. When Julian started seventh grade at this private school, he had the right environment, which included small classes and one-on-one instruction, plus tutoring to learn how to focus better and compensate for his learning disabilities without the need for meds. He began to see where he needed to slow down and focus more. It was very valuable for Julian to have such skilled and caring teachers who were used to working with twice-exceptional kids like him. He was able to catch up in subjects he'd been falling behind in, and he was able to explore some of his talents in music and drama by being in the school musical presentation.

With school going better, I could support his passions more. I'd read that the key for gifted kids was to help them find their passion, so I enrolled Julian in drumming classes because he had shown great interest in music, had studied tuba and French horn with excitement, and wanted to be a drummer. He was also influenced tremendously by his friends who were starting rock bands and playing music. So he started drumming in his new band of cohorts with rehearsals at the other band members' homes after school and on weekends. He was on his way to finding a healing path with his music.

My new life as a family therapist and divorced single mom continued to inform my private practice. I had to leave the office in Longmont where I was dealing with so much divorce because I no longer believed in the work I was doing with divorcing and divorced people. I had my foot in both worlds: I was a parent of divorce and I was also a professional treating parents of divorce. I was living the challenges, and it was putting me under unnecessary strain as a professional. I had to shift my practice. As I asked myself what was next, I realized that I wanted to help women find resilience through menopause and midlife challenges like divorce. It made much more sense to me to strengthen a woman's ability to stay healthy and balanced than to wait until illness showed up. I still wanted to work with families too, but I wanted to drop divorce cases.

I decided to move my practice closer to home, and I found the right situation in Gunbarrel, an unincorporated area of Boulder Country that was halfway between Longmont and Boulder. I was excited to join a new group of therapists starting an integrative family therapeutic and wellness center designed for special needs families and adoptive families. My new practice had a meeting room for us to use for groups as well as a very exciting variety of modalities to offer our clients including play therapy, speech and occupational therapy, naturopathy, psychological testing, family therapy, individual trauma therapies, and classes for parents. The location would accommodate my current clients and allow me to expand into more connecting communities to the east of Boulder as well as offer more groups and workshops.

One of the best wellness tools out there for personal resourcing and growth at that time was mindfulness. Since I had begun to read about mindfulness and was exploring it in yoga, I was learning how it could help with my depression and stress. I picked up Jon Kabat-Zinn's book, *Full Catastrophe Living*, on his mindfulness-based stress reduction (MBSR) program at the University of Massachusetts and read it thoroughly. I also read *Mindsight* by Daniel Siegal. Those books showed me how mindfulness was the tool I was looking for to help myself and other women find wholeness and healing.

I decided to attend Kabat-Zinn's MBSR training program for therapists at Mt. Madonna retreat center in California when I could free myself from the day-to-day challenges with Julian. I wanted to teach that work, but until I could get away to take that training, I had another option. The Shambhala Mountain Center in Boulder offered an introductory class in MBSR, and I signed up for that. There I would begin to learn more about my stress and how to slow down my mind. Janet's voice was so soothing that first morning in class. She started with sitting meditation. "Feel the body as a whole. Strong back; soft front."

She had us bring our attention to how the breath was naturally occurring in our bodies, and she asked us to allow our attention to ride the breath on every complete inhalation and exhalation. I noticed how calming it was to slowly let my attention ride the breath, especially as it ended the exhalation and started the next inhalation.

She led us slowly and deliberately, allowing time to lapse between the components of her instruction so we could follow along in a relaxed way. "There are moments when you notice you are distracted and your mind is not on the breath. You notice you are thinking of the present and of the past. Sometimes it's emotions, drama, memories, feelings, or thoughts. Just acknowledge all those things as distractions coming from the mind and come back to the breath."

I was seeing that my mind did exactly what she was pointing out, and it was such a relief to have her name it all.

"Develop the courage to see what arises in the mind and the body. And with an unconditional attitude, just notice it and let it go as you exhale. Every time we let go, we counteract the tendency to cling to thoughts, feelings, and sensations. Using your breath as your object, stay awake, clear, and stable, coming back to the breath in each moment."

It all made sense to me intellectually. That's what I was doing. I was clinging to thoughts, feelings, and sensations and letting them overwhelm me. When I let them go through my body with my breath, they flowed through me. It was enlightening.

But getting that process into my body was only the beginning. My intellect wanted to manage it all as I had done for so much of my life. Slowly, though, the class and the mindfulness practices of sitting meditation, walking meditation, and body scan began to teach me how to pay more attention to my body and what was happening there and how to notice how my feelings showed up. I began to learn how I reacted to feelings and thoughts, which was more stressful than just noticing they were there and allowing them. I was learning how to develop curiosity and courage so I could pay attention in a whole new way through my senses and my body instead of just through my intellect or my mind.

That was the beginning of learning the tools and process needed to go down into my feelings and get a sense of what my body had to say. It was called *embodiment*, and it was another important mooring—a way for me to anchor and stabilize myself in the present moment.

Chapter Six

Reclaiming Family

I WAS HEADED TO Denver International Airport with Julian for a flight to Winter Haven, Florida, my hometown, where we would be spending Thanksgiving vacation. On the way, I dropped by the Boulder Bookstore to get a book to read while on my vacation. *Internal Family Systems Therapy* by Richard Schwartz jumped off the shelf and into my hands. As I continued on to the airport, I started wondering about the title. Was the author talking about family members as "parts" within us? I dove into the book during the flight and saw that he was, indeed, talking about parts inside us, and I realized that I already saw different parts inside my clients and myself. I thought he was on to something, and I hoped he could tell me how to work with those parts.

The discovery of that book and its insights triggered two beginnings: One was a totally new phase of my life as a psychotherapist. The second was the beginning of my path toward personal healing of trauma I didn't even know was there.

Since the divorce, Julian and I had been visiting my Florida family twice a year, which was more frequently than before, and we always made a trip to Florida for Thanksgiving. That was the best time for me to see all of my siblings and for Julian to hang out with all of his cousins. We both needed that kind of connection with larger family and friends to feel comfort and support.

That fall, my mom and dad, now in their late seventies, had downsized from our family home on Eagle Lake to a smaller home with a pool. My dad had been dealing with painful and debilitating arthritis in his back as well as Parkinson's disease and couldn't do stairs anymore, so the new home was all on one level. Mom had wanted us to stay with them at the new home, though it was much smaller. It was a bit awkward for Julian and me, but I realized I needed to help make the new place comfortable for us, so I made a makeshift bedroom for us in the home office by pulling in a mattress and covering the windows.

I was glad I was there because I was able to help out my mom and dad and get to know the part-time caregivers supporting them. The afternoon of our arrival, Mom took Julian and me around the new house and showed us the pool and yard. Then we went into the little cottage on the grounds that had been used for entertaining but now was used for storage. The cottage immediately became the playhouse. Julian's cousin, Marjorie, lived in Florida, and she got to her grandmother's house just as we arrived, so the three of us began exploring the cottage.

Mom sat on a lawn chair and watched as Julian and Marjorie pulled out innertubes, balls, and foam noodle floats that had been stored in the cottage and used them to create a fort outside on the grass. They played with the fort for a time and then left it to jump into the pool. The cousins were very close, possibly because my sister and I had both experienced divorces and made a point of getting them together whenever Julian and I came to Florida. They had a lot in common, and they teased and taunted each other in their play, but they did so more lovingly than if they were siblings.

The relationship between the cousins was very different from how my sister, Martha, and I had related as kids. There were seven kids in our family, and Martha and I had sometimes viciously attacked one another to get attention. Where there had been too much competition between Martha and me growing up, there was just a desire to be connected between Julian and Marjorie.

As they were swimming, I stepped back and let Mom supervise, which was what she wanted to do. Without being asked, she was always at the ready to take over for me when I visited. "Mom, what are you going to do with the cottage?" I asked, wondering about the upkeep because it needed some work.

"I don't know yet. Right now it's serving a purpose." She pointed to the kids, and I knew she was happy to have them making use of the new property and having fun. She was living in the present moment.

I told her I loved the pool and yard and asked if she minded if I checked out things. She was fine with that, so I left the kids at her watch and wandered over to the garage, which was on the other side of the pool. Beautiful azaleas were blooming along the pool and all kinds of tropical plants were hanging in pots. I'd forgotten how everything stayed so beautiful in Florida all through the winter. I breathed in the smells and warmth of Florida, so familiar to my younger self, who had grown up there.

When I reached the garage, I saw Dad tinkering with kids' bicycles. He was fixing them up so the kids could ride them.

"How's your back feeling doing this?" I asked.

"I just don't have as much in me, Donna, but I can still tinker a bit," he replied.

He had a bike upside down with the seat on the ground, and I watched him flip it back upright and test the brakes. He managed to maneuver pretty well from a small stool to standing without having to lean over very much. I wondered how debilitated he'd feel later, but like Mom, he was happy in this present moment being a grandparent. Both of them seemed to drop into that soft spot of their lives quite comfortably whenever they got the chance. Mom even created it by inviting everyone over as much as possible, even though they had downsized into a smaller home. She was allowing more help now, with the support of my sisters, Martha and Ellen, being close by to hire caregivers. They wanted to be independent, but it was time to let go a bit, and I was pleased to see that.

I thanked my dad for getting the bikes together and went back to the pool area. "Papa has some bikes fixed up you both can ride in the neighborhood if you'd like to."

Marj turned to Julian with a huge mischievous smile on her face. "Let's go, Jules!" She jumped out of the pool and pulled a towel around her as she barreled over to the garage in her bare feet. Julian was immediately behind her, both of them running without shoes.

That moment reminded me of how much fun we had as kids riding bikes together in the circle drive at our home on Eagle Lake. With a family of seven kids, there was always a hand-me-down bike that an older brother or sister had used. Since I was one of the big kids, I usually got a new bike, scooter, or skates, but the younger kids usually got hand-me-downs unless we'd already destroyed the equipment. Sometimes, though, the younger kids got something entirely new that hadn't been used by anyone before them.

I played with my brothers often, and we were pretty tough on bikes and trikes because we rode them into the dirt driveway and tried to go farther than they could go in the soft sand. Then we'd get frustrated and leave them there—for which we got in trouble.

As we got older, I was the most skilled at balance and learning new tricks, and I taught myself to ride a unicycle I received for Christmas. Starting off by holding onto the car door handle, I would pedal across the side of the car and then back again until I felt secure enough to set off across the cement driveway to the next car. One day, Dad came home with pogo sticks, and I jumped and jumped on them until I was exhausted. My energy carried me through, but my energy also sometimes got me in trouble. Julian was a lot like me in that way.

I helped Julian pick out the bike that best fit him, and though it was a bit small for him, he was determined to ride it. He rode a small mountain bike in Boulder, so he was looking for big fat tires, but these were pretty thin. His legs were dragging, so we raised the seat to fit him better. Marjorie jumped on the pink bike that Papa had fixed up for her, and they headed out of the garage before I could catch up with them.

I ran down the street yelling at Marjorie to slow down and watch for cars. I had to grab her seat and slow her down as Julian came screeching to a stop with his well-lubricated brakes. "You two have to follow the rules and stop at all intersections. Marj, this is a busy street. You know how to be careful on your bike, right?"

She looked at me cross-eyed, and I saw a bit of her wildness flashing. She was a very spirited child, and when she and Julian were together, it was a lot of work to keep them contained.

"Julian doesn't know this neighborhood yet, and you have to show him how carefully you've learned to ride here. This is not like in the groves where the other house was. It's more dangerous here. Do you hear me?" I looked right into her eyes and got my head down to her level. Julian was aware of my tone and got quiet.

They got back on their bikes and rode a route that would bring them behind the house and away from the traffic. That felt relatively safe to me. When they got back, I let them know that was the route to stay on. They both agreed and took off for a second loop. Mom walked toward me as I was heading to the front of the house. "Those two are always a handful," I mused shaking my head.

"Donna, it just goes with the territory. You were just like that!"

She'd said exactly what I'd been thinking, but somehow it hadn't felt so good when she said it. I switched topics. "Remember that catfish float-boat fishing trip you took them on when they were both six? You were a saint to do that!"

She grimaced then smiled back at me. "We had so much fun even though it was exhausting!"

We connected as equals as we remembered the experience together. I was seeing the image of Julian and Marjorie running around the deck of a huge float boat on Lake Hatchineha in wild central Florida, playing instead of fishing, talking to the captain and playing with the bait. Mom had wanted to share her love of fishing with Julian and Marjorie, her most energetic grandchildren, by hiring the boat and captain. That was my mom at her greatest generous self, offering an adventure but maybe not realizing how much work that kind of fishing trip might be for her.

I was glad I went along because the kids needed a lot of supervision to help them stay focused enough to catch a fish. And both were successful at it because of Mom's perseverance and patience with them. It was a great day in the beauty of Florida's natural wetlands. My heart warmed at the memory of that outrageously adventurous outing I'd loved doing with her. It had taken a toll on her, but she brushed it off as nothing because she had given the kids the experience of a lifetime. Being with her grandkids fully was a huge priority for her, and I suspected she enjoyed her grandkids much more than she'd enjoyed her own children when we were growing up. As soon as we were no longer babies, we got less attention and more discipline. Hence the infighting and competition.

I was knocked out of my reverie by Marjorie speeding by. And then she jumped off her bike, letting it fall where it landed, and headed for the pool again. Julian followed her lead, and before I could get to the garage, they were gone. Mom headed into the house to check on dinner.

That first afternoon and evening of our Thanksgiving visit was the best part of that trip. I treasured being with my parents and the kids at that important time of transition for them. It seemed better than earlier times, maybe because I was so far away and our visits were less frequent, or maybe because Mom knew time was going by and life was short. I was reclaiming the parts of my life in Florida that I treasured and holding them dear in what was also a time of transition for me. And I realized that transitions, whether chosen or forced on us, created times for us to stop and notice so much.

In the early hours when I woke up and looked over at Julian sleeping so deeply, I sat and listened quietly inside. In those moments, I began to notice my younger parts, the ones that always came out when I went back home. I was learning how to observe them as "parts" instead of all of me, thanks to reading *Internal Family Systems Therapy*. When I observed them that way, I had the ability to see my strong parts—like the courageous adult woman dealing with my transition, the therapist part, the mother of a gifted child, and the lost wife. I saw the open heart part of me that gave so much to others, and I realized I was seeing a similar part in my mother during the visit.

I was changing inside. It wasn't about needing my parents' guidance anymore. It wasn't about leaning on my husband anymore. I was a grown up, and I felt it. I had newfound solidity, determination, and perseverance, and those strengths allowed me to nudge up against the vulnerable feelings in my broken-ness brought on by the divorce. I had begun to explore my inner feelings and reactions and learn how to face them and be curi-ous about them instead of judging them and pushing them aside. I was finding another mooring.

I was learning how to do that in my parenting, in my work, and in my own therapy and mindfulness practice. By sitting with myself mindfully and allowing and accepting whatever was there, I was learning how to let go of the rigidity about who I wanted to be and how I wanted to be treated and loved. And I was more able to accept the present goodness in my life.

Later, I would be able to identify the parts of me that had held rigidity in so many of my relationships and then shift it more permanently.

Chapter Seven

Befriending My Parts

AFTER THE VISIT TO FLORIDA, I looked for training in Internal Family Systems (IFS), and I was able to enroll in a Level I training that was to be offered over eight weekends the following April. And it was being held in Boulder for the first time, which made it affordable for me to attend. I signed up and continued to read and prepare for learning the model through the experiential training program.

In the months following Thanksgiving, I read and studied everything I could find about the different trauma therapies coming out, and I did some initial workshops in Somatic Experiencing. Most trauma techniques were about bringing regulation and healing to the body and specifically, to the autonomic nervous system. I learned that a dysregulated nervous system was typically an indication of trauma, so reestablishing regulation was an important part of healing and resilience going forward. Those learnings trickled through me, and I became more curious about my own dysregulation when I got upset or excited, which were the result of situations pushing me past my window of tolerance and being unable to get back in balance quickly.

I was becoming more aware of parts I had inside me that were still raw from my divorce, and I was curious about how to heal them. I realized that listening to what was inside me using the IFS process would help me see what that healing needed to be. I could be in charge of my own healing process, and that was very exciting to me. In the IFS model, unhealed parts—parts that had been traumatized or injured in some way—created a burdened system. And a burdened system was one that was shut down, had less energy, and was unable to reach its full potential. But by using IFS, those unhealed parts could be recognized and healed, unburdening the system. The IFS model was based on a transpersonal healing process I found empowering because it was based on the concept that we hold all the healing and loving energy of the Divine/Infinite/Oneness (whatever word worked for a person to describe the life force of creativity in the universe) inside us. And all we needed to do was tap into it within us to heal ourselves. That greater goodness inside us was what Richard Schwartz called the *Self*.

Besides healing myself with the process, learning to use IFS with my clients revolutionized my therapy practice. I no longer felt I had to fix my clients when they came to me feeling broken. Now I had a way of working with clients that allowed *me* to see their wholeness and guide *them* to find that wholeness, from which they could heal themselves. I became more a guide, facilitator, and coach than a therapist. It was less burdensome and more empowering to me because it fit my belief system about working from strengths rather than weaknesses.

It felt more therapeutic when it was time to go down deeper into the client's inner system where the very young parts were. That happened later in the IFS process after all the "manager" parts (worker bee parts that had important jobs to keep a person successful in the world) were identified, appreciated, and understood as part of the whole system. Those younger parts were called the "exiles" because they had been exiled early in life into roles that didn't serve them—like caretaker, victim, or rescuer roles or as depressed or shut down gifted parts. Healing those exiles felt like a kind of spiritual soul retrieval in a deep ritualistic process that allowed them to be unburdened and freed up to be whole, alive, and vital again in the person's system. I was really curious about my own exiles and how they might be burdened.

That spring and summer, I completed my first two training weekends with the IFS Level 1 trainers and was meeting the others in the program. I was told I needed to start individual therapy with an IFS therapist as I moved through the training program, and I couldn't wait to break open my internal system and learn more. Soon I began to meet with Barb, a movement therapist and IFS trainer, as my personal therapist, and I loved working with her. She called herself a somatic (body-focused) IFS therapist.

One day not long after another visit with my family in Florida, I wanted to talk with her about how it felt to see my mom love Julian so unconditionally. I was curious about the conflict it set up inside me between the parent/adult part that needed my mom's support in the present and the "little girl" parts that were holding a lot of resentment and anger about my relationship with my mom from my childhood.

I sat down in a turquoise-cushioned loveseat in Barb's makeshift therapy room/art studio in her rustic home near Hygiene. It was refreshing to get out into the farmland north of Boulder, even though the drive to her office took twenty minutes. I was fascinated by the art supplies behind her and her tiny, delicate paintings and folk art pieces hanging on portable screens covering her art table. Barb was a very creative, gifted individual, and she was a good match for me.

When she walked in and greeted me, her dark eyes caught mine with a questioning and loving look. Then she started the session by asking what had brought me in. I told her I had just come back from visiting my mom, and a lot of my parts were coming up.

"Can you get in touch with the part of you that is screaming right now?" she asked.

I closed my eyes, which I had learned to do when I went inside to feel a part. It was the inner work of being curious about a part and sensing it by going down into your body. Sometimes parts were outside the body, but mine seemed to be either in my head or physically in my body. "She's wanting to let out her feelings of anger and resentment about my mom. She's so overwhelming."

"How do you feel toward her, Donna?"

"I don't like her. I want her to go away because she scares me."

"Which part is scared of her?"

"Oh, that's the one that hates my emotional one and pushes her away." I opened my eyes in a squint to see Barb writing on her tablet and thought about how the scared part was part of my protective system. That was the thinking part of me reflecting, and it continued in my head. *We just learned about that in our second training weekend. The protective system is comprised of parts that keep us safe and functional in the world and in our families, and they work hard for our success.* I reclosed my eyes and refocused internally with a deep breath, noticing that my thinking part was trying to take over.

"What are you noticing now?

"I just went into my thinking part who had to tell me all about the protective system and I'm curious why she did that?

"Can you ask her? Barb asked.

I turned my attention inward and had a conversation with my thinking part before answering Barb. "Yes. She has to keep me from getting overwhelmed and too emotional. She helps me figure out everything so I can be safe. So does the other part, the scared one. They are both showing me how it's not safe to be emotional because I'll upset everyone, especially my mom."

"How are you feeling toward those protector parts?"

"I need them. I'm curious. I like that they help me manage my emotions more." I paused for a moment. "I can get really big sometimes."

"Who gets really big sometimes?" Barb asked.

"My emotional one. Oh, yeah. She just did it again. I get pulled into being her so much. Can you help me not be so blended with her?" I was noticing how I lost the perspective of my present self when I went down and connected with those younger, exiled parts.

"So you are noticing that you get pulled out of Self by her, that she sort of takes you over? What if you just breathe in more Self energy so you can expand the space between you and her?" She paused for a moment to scribble some notes. "How do you feel toward her now that you see her?"

"I'm curious, and I feel her settling some."

"Can you ask those parts that are uncomfortable to just step back for few moments? We only have about five minutes left, and I'll help you go slowly to just peek at her. What does she want to show you?

"Too much emotion there. She's crying and screaming at the same time. I can't stay that close. I get scared."

"So when you start to get close to her, your protectors come in and block you from being with her. Is that right?" Barb asked.

"Yes. Now that you say it, I see that. I guess we have to get to know the protectors more, especially the one who's scared of her, because she won't let me connect with the emotional one."

In the following sessions, Barb helped me continue to go inside my internal system and befriend the major protector (manager) as my doer/achiever/thinker who worked really hard to help me be seen as good, smart, and successful—for instance, as a good daughter, a smart woman, and a successful therapist. Her fear and belief was that when I was emotional, I would create chaos, become dysregulated with too much emotion, and be unable to settle down, which would interfere with my relationships and my ability to be successful in my life. She believed that because I had been like that as a baby and as a young girl, I would still get emotionally overwhelmed sometimes.

I learned that my "protective system" had strong managers, including a perfectionist and a critical/judging part that were modeled after my mother and father to keep me on the straight and narrow. They held back the emotional parts (my exiles or younger parts) to avoid more pain to them. I was really curious about what had caused them pain. Each time I got a peek at them, they were less scary to me and to my protectors. I wanted to know what happened between my mother and me that had caused me to feel so much dread.

But more important at the moment was how calm my system slowly got when I talked to my managers and they began to trust me. The intensity dissipated. The managers began to trust that I was there to love and care for all my parts because I learned to treat them with curiosity and compassion. That made IFS healing for me. I could bring compassion inward as I explored and befriended each of my parts, and it created more and more peace and calm inside.

Slowly, I understood more about what I felt as conflict inside. My intensity was just my protective system holding down my exiles (emotional little girl parts) that needed to be heard and allowed to have their feelings. When I was critical of myself because something had gone wrong or I pushed too hard to correct something, my emotional parts were exiled even deeper by my managers to cut off any connection with them. I had to rebalance my internal system by freeing the exiles or unburdening them—letting them tell me their stories and release their feelings. That shift would allow the protective system to let go, see that something had changed, and allow more connection and love to flow internally with the parts. More self-compassion could grow inside me. This was the goal and I was on my way with my IFS personal therapy.

Over the next few years of personal therapy work, I learned about my early attachment injuries during the first two years of my life, which had caused distrust in relationships with others as well as in my relationship with myself. It took several years before I could really befriend my exiles because my system needed a lot of time to feel my love and trust me—which was an indication that my ability to develop healthy attachment had been challenged at an early age. My burdened protective system treated me inside a bit like my family. I felt I needed to shut down my emotional parts. Inside, my parts had modeled the way my family behaved.

Going slowly was the only way to create a more secure attachment with myself and my parts. That was also what IFS could offer me. It was a way to re-parent myself and my parts and heal my attachment injuries. I didn't need another relationship right then. I needed to be in relationship with myself more deeply. That was the healing I needed to do first.

I was able to journal and draw some of my parts, and I slowly released some of the confusion of anger, fear, sadness, and despair that lurked in my stomach and chest, which was where those parts resided in my body. The process of embodying my feelings again happened slowly because I had pushed them away for so long. Luckily, I was exploring other ways to release feel-ings in my body through yoga, dance, and meditation. All those things contributed to the process of healing and coming to wholeness that IFS had begun for me.

My embodiment had begun.

Chapter Eight

My Fierce and Wise
Feminine Parts

TWO DAYS AFTER CHRISTMAS, I got an emergency phone call from my sister, Martha, who was closely overseeing my mom and dad in their home. Mom had experienced a serious stroke in the middle of the night, and she'd been rushed to the hospital, where she was in intensive care. She suffered paralysis on the whole right side of her body, and they weren't sure how much she would be able to recover.

I wanted to fly home, but Martha assured me that I should not come yet. I stayed in touch by phone, and within the week, Mom was recovering and was going to be moved to a recovery facility that could help her get the physical therapy and occupational therapy she needed. I was able to talk with her on the phone, and she reassured me that I should stay in Colorado.

The reports coming from Florida throughout her recovery period were varied, but my sisters and brothers were all very engaged in working together to get her better and back home. Meanwhile, my dad continued to live at home with his regular caregivers helping him with his daily living tasks.

Mom recovered some use of her right side and was able to eat and talk somewhat, but she was unable to do more than that with her body. The staff at the recovery center said she needed to work harder to be able to walk again. I talked with the doctors and Martha, and it seemed she had given up hope about being able to walk again. The stroke had impacted her emotional expression, and even though she could still talk, she spoke very softly and without emotion. They called it "emotional blunting." Otherwise, her cognitive capacity and thinking were normal. That was a blessing. She came home in March, and it seemed her life would continue in a wheelchair.

I didn't realize the impact it was having on me. That close call was a powerful sign of what was to come, but I was too distracted with my current struggles to really notice. So I didn't go to Florida after the stroke. I couldn't seem to get my attention off my own stuff to pay attention to just how much my mom was declining. Her steadfast support had been a lifesaver to me since my divorce, and she had been so involved with the grandchildren that my mind became stuck on who she'd been instead of who she had become.

I planned to see my mother in June, but she had another stroke, a small one, in May. She'd lost consciousness, her vital signs were at a dangerous level, and she'd been rushed to the hospital. I knew I needed to go to Florida then, not in a couple of weeks. Peter was going to spend some time with Julian anyway, and he agreed to take him early. The way was being made clear for me to see my mother.

My older sister Ellen met me at the airport, and on the way to the hospital, I asked her how Mom was doing.

"I think she's about the same, but it's still touch-and-go," she said, keeping her eyes on the road. She seemed to be holding her emotions tightly, though I could tell she was distraught. Ellen was the most emotionally available of my siblings, and I loved that about her.

We met Martha and my brothers at the hospital, and while they all gave me the token hug, I could feel everyone's tension.

I wondered if Mom was near the end, which felt scary, but I couldn't let my mind go there. When I entered Mom's room and embraced Dad, who had been sitting in a chair next to her, he seemed shaken. Mom was unnaturally pale, but she managed to smile with the left side of her face. Her hazel eyes were trying to sparkle at me, like they always had, but something was way different. It felt as if her extroverted, social self was gone and what was left was just the shell of her.

"Hi, sweetie," she said. "Are you tired from your long trip here?"

She'd always been a great caretaker, but it seemed inappropriate in that moment.

"Mom, I'm here because I want to help you get back on your feet. This second stroke isn't going to slow you down, is it?"

"I hope not," she replied, but there was a dropping off of her words and her energy.

Dad asked if she was up to seeing the kids, and while she said she was fine with that, I wasn't so sure. I wondered if she was in denial about the severity of her situation or if it was just her typical stoicism talking.

That afternoon we all gathered with Dad in their new home to have a late lunch, and as I looked out at the pool area, I realized it would be a great place for Mom to do her physical therapy once she got out of the hospital and discovered that my siblings had already suggested it to the physical therapists.

Martha and I had planned a trip to England and Spain with her sixteen-year-old daughter, and we were scheduled to leave in four days, but with Mom not even stabilized, I realized we would probably have to cancel the trip and admitted that to Martha.

"Let's take it a day at a time, Donna," she replied. "I agree it's a possibility we may have to cancel, but we need to see how she does in the next few days. The doctors say she needs to have the will to get back into that wheelchair and work on her body."

"But she almost gave up the first time. With this new setback, I'm worried she'll lose hope."

"That's why you're here, Donna," Martha admitted. "We all need to let her know we want her to get better."

I could feel the fear rolling through my chest, the familiar fear I felt when new and scary things happened in my life. I'd felt it on a rock ledge as I waited to take my next pitch of a rock climb with Peter. I'd felt it when I was all alone trying to nurse Julian as a newborn. And I'd felt it when my sister, Marjorie, had been in a bad car accident and was fighting for her life. Those memories flashed through my brain and body, and then the fear overtook me. "But what if she doesn't get better? What are her chances?"

Martha answered matter-of-factly. "We can't tell. The doctors say it's up to her."

There was such a plethora of numbness in the room that I had to get up and walk outdoors. Even my Dad seemed shut down, and that was unusual for him.

When Marjorie died after a car accident, my father cried visibly and openly in front of us as he talked about his feelings for her. While I was numb with shock and grief, he had openly expressed his deep grief. My mother was unable to grieve or even cry. She was sick with a cold at the time and remained isolated in her room while the rest of the family sat together downstairs and tried to grieve. And she was sick for weeks.

The experience of my sister's death had helped me see how feelings were mostly shut down in all of us. Instead of feeling, our default position was to figure out and fix things. My parents handled grief in very different ways, and I realized I wanted to let out my feelings and let them cleanse and heal me like they had for my father instead of burying them as my mother did. My father's free expression of grief gave me permission to start freeing and expressing my own feelings as I moved on from that experience.

Seeing my mom's emotional blunting after the second stroke worried me. For someone who already held her feelings back and pushed them down, a stroke's impact could be devastating. I wondered how she was feeling inside with a mangled and twisted body that needed help to do the simplest of things. Nobody was talking about that. Didn't she need to talk about it instead of being stuck inside her body alone?

I had opened up my curiosity to look at my mother more deeply and more compassionately than I had in the past. Somehow, I'd been able to move past the resentment I'd felt toward her in my early twenties that had led to my move to Colorado. She had been there for me during my postpartum crisis and in the years following my divorce, and she had been a wonderful and loving grandmother to my child.

Now I was able to hold my heart more open for her. I wondered if my own struggles and pain had played a part in my ability to view her with compassion, and in that moment, I realized I had a big capacity for compassion. I also realized that compassion for others had been modeled for me by my mom, even though she never seemed to have that same compassion for herself. She had a huge heart and cared for others deeply—including me. Because of the stroke, Mom was going to get some help working with self-compassion and learning how to bring it inward, something many women didn't learn until late in life because they were taught to care for others before themselves. Like many women, my mother was well trained to be a martyr.

Melissa, one of the regular caregivers, was selected to spend overnights with Mom when she returned home, and Melissa was the most loving person I had ever met. I had gotten the opportunity to spend time with her on my last visit, and I'd seen how much she loved everyone and how much of herself she gave to others. Melissa saw how my mother presented a tough veneer, resisting self-care and self-love and even having difficulty accepting the compassion my siblings and I were showing her. All of that made Melissa the perfect caregiver to help Mom develop a little compassion for herself.

Mom pulled herself back from the edge. In only a few days, she was well enough to get back into her wheelchair and go home to a new life with a wheelchair and a full-time caregiver.

My sister and I did make our trip to England and Spain, and it wasn't until I returned and settled back into my usual routine that I realized the impact of seeing my mother's diminished state—not only on my usual "self," but also on all of the family parts inside me that I was starting to meet in my IFS work.

Grief about my mother's condition and what it meant to me rose up and poured out of me. I was able to process it, but other things were coming forward too.

◇   ◇   ◇

I'd just finished up with a client and had changed into yoga clothes in preparation for a therapeutic kundalini-style yoga class being offered by my colleague and friend, Arielle. She was offering the classes to her office mates until she felt ready to expand them to more clients and the public, and we were using the same meeting room I used for group sessions and classes.

I was grateful because I needed a "body break," as I called the exercise or physical activities at midday that brought me into my body and out of my head and my work. We started with brief check-ins. Arielle's soft, gentle music and her encouraging voice lulled me into my body and out of my head as I rolled out my mat and sat down.

We started with breathing and kundalini centering, and I moved my breath up and down my chakras, clearing and noticing what was there. I had become fascinated with the chakras thanks to a guided meditation I had listened to a few years earlier, and I had been learning about yoga—reading everything I could find on Hindu mythology and the science of yoga—as well as taking yoga classes in Boulder, which was a hotbed of yoga and other Eastern practices. Moving mindfulness, as yoga was called, was sometimes easier for me than sitting practices.

Yoga was all about bringing prana, or life force, through the body, starting at the root chakra with the kundalini energy that came from the goddess of the feminine called Shakti and represented the feminine in power and energy that moved along our sacred channel in the spine. Shakti, nestled in the first or root chakra, joined through the breath with Shiva, the masculine principle coming from the consciousness center at the seventh or crown chakra. When those two energies came together at the fourth chakra, the heart center in the body, they created oneness—a true awakening of our divine nature inside us.

Yoga theory aligned well with the concept of the larger Self and the spiritual healing aspects of IFS. Awakening the chakras by practicing yoga was bringing in this life force, this Divine Feminine kundalini energy, and embodying it. I found this yogic teaching helpful as I allowed myself to be curious about what I was experiencing inside.

"Slowly roll your hips in a circle. Very gently inhale as you move forward. Exhale as you roll back."

Arielle's loving tone drew me into my body in a curious way. I loved waking up my hips and how doing so made my body start to relax. I realized that I probably held a lot of stuff in my hips, and I tuned into the practice more deeply. "Now begin to tip your pelvis forward and backwards, moving your torso forward and back, breathing in and breathing out, releasing any tension in your neck and head, letting them follow the movement. That's right."

I let my body start moving, guided by my pubic bone, pulling up toward my belly button and my sacrum, rocking forward and letting my pelvis drop forward as I watched Arielle's pelvis doing the same rocking motion. There were only four of us in class, so we had lots of room to go inward. I began to tune into my breathing, and since the mirrors were covered with curtains, I couldn't see myself or others reflected. That encouraged me to focus inward more. We were all undulating our upper torsos up into our shoulders, holding the tops of our shoulders with our hands, twisting them from side to side with each inhalation and exhalation.

That went on until I couldn't wait for her to tell us to stop.

"Let's get our energy moving now. Ready for some Kapalbhati Pranayama or Breath of Fire, reaching your arms out with thumbs up. It's done by pumping the naval point toward the spine on the exhale and releasing the naval out on the inhale."

She demonstrated by puffing short breaths, and we all followed her. I felt suspended in time, totally present and alive. My arms felt bright and shiny, and I slowly began to feel that warming energy rising in my belly. Suddenly, I felt some sensations rising up in my heart area too. I noticed the tension around those sensations as they rose up, and I noticed tears coming to my eyes. Sadness? I wondered where it was from.

I let myself move into the next pose, letting Arielle's voice move to the background as I stayed connected to the emotions rising up. Curious, I tuned inward more. It was about my mom and how she was vanishing from my life, how she looked like a shell of herself after the stroke. I kept moving and breathing as more tears welled up.

"Just come to Table Top and slowly inhale as you reach into Cow Pose, extending your spine. Now slowly exhale as you pull your chin and your focus inward. Following your breath, what do you notice?"

I couldn't control the tears, so I just moved through them, releasing more and more emotions as I undulated until my mat was covered with tears. I went more inward, feeling safe as Arielle guided me.

"That's it. Just let it flow. Whatever needs to happen, you're safe here."

I was able to tune in to what those feelings were trying to release, knowing my friends in the room would understand. I was safe to explore the moment there.

I couldn't quite follow the next directions, so I dropped down on my belly and moved into Cobra, then Down Dog, trying to catch up with the group. Holding and breathing in Down Dog Pose, I was able to calibrate and feel some acceptance with my feelings. Yoga was helping me process, and I felt huge sensations well up in my heart area. I extended my right leg on cue and stepped forward into a Crescent Lunge, finding my grounding slowly, hands on hips. I steadied myself and carefully dropped into my strong legs and feet, that familiar feeling of getting grounded that I loved to come back to. I was getting more present again with her directions and feeling safer to attend to the sensations in my heart.

"Just let yourself drop deeper into the earth, grounding your body in this pose, finding your inner strength from your inner thighs pulling together. That's right. Now, straightening your back leg, reach your arms up up. That's it. And now lower them gently, right arm in front, left arm to the back as you press your hips forward, dropping gently into lunge, Warrior II. Good. Now, inhale, and exhale slowly."

As we paused there, thoughts began to pour into my mind again. *My mom has been such an enigma for me. I was so angry with her, and I so admired her too.* Then I noticed how much I wanted to push the confusion away. Then sadness cried out, and I tried to listen, but my body wanted to push past it into a Triangle Pose. Slowly, moving my body there, I touched my left hand to the top of my right shin as I reached my right arm straight up, wavering, and tears began to drop from my eyes. I noticed a great tightness in my heart chakra. As my leg dropped into a lunge, I wanted to drop into Sleeping Pigeon Pose and feel my heart more. As I did that, Arielle directed us all to go there. I hung my head over my right leg, which was bent into a forty-five-degree angle under me. I extended my left leg back, turning my toe down into the earth as I pressed onto my right hip joint and felt a twinge of pain. That hip was tight, so I eased off a little.

Breathing gently, I let my awareness go to my heart and my hips. What was there? My left leg slipped back an inch, and I hung over and cupped my chin with my right wrist. Noticing more tears, I opened up to them.

Then I realized I was back in my mind, time traveling to my postpartum depression, then to my divorce, and then to how my mother tried to move past her discomfort with me to love me more. I didn't want to go there again, but I was curiously drawn deeper. Deep tingling sensations rolled through my heart and down to my root chakra, deep in my pelvis. Finally, I took them in, curious and ignited by them. I was starting to allow those feelings to be there and accept the deep knowing I was feeling.

We moved into a twist, and I relaxed and breathed, opening more deeply into the release. We pressed back into Down Dog, and then we slowly moved to the other side for Sleeping

Pigeon. As my mind began to quiet more, I felt my heart more than my hips. I felt an opening and a clarity about my deep capacity for love and my longing to be connected deeply to others I loved. I hadn't felt that before so clearly.

I stopped and breathed into my heart, savoring the intensity of that love at last. I didn't have to fix or do anything with it—just feel it. I felt peaceful as I allowed myself to drop into a more accepting and loving place with myself.

I decided to let my body finish the class and not go back to any thinking. My body knew what to do. I let go into the deep release of my right hip. That took me to a calmer, more connected place, and I felt gratitude as I swung my leg into a twist to one side. I was trusting myself and letting go into the wisdom of my body.

Then we rolled out into forward folds. Sitting tall on my sit bones with my legs straight in front of me, I gently moved my heart closer to my legs, keeping my back straight until I needed to curl it to embrace my legs, nose to my shins. There was nothing to do but let go. It was so comforting. I was suddenly loving myself and my body's strength and flexibility. I'd done that stretch for so many years that my body and I had a very special connection when I did it.

"Now, just let go into Savasana," Arielle said as the music became fainter and slower. The sound of a cello pulled me into its sweetness, and I drifted off completely into a soft slumber.

Chapter Nine

Starting Over

ONE MORNING BEFORE JULIAN AWOKE, I was sitting quietly on my meditation cushion in the corner of my bedroom which I had set up as my sacred space. In *A Room of One's Own*, Virginia Woolf said it was important to have personal space, and I had come to understand that having an altar on which I placed meaningful objects that represented the best of me anchored my energies and ritualized my connection with my deeper self. But while my study of self-care had led me to the concept of sacred space, it took a long time for me to incorporate it into my daily routine. It had taken being on my own in my own house—my own space—to feel how the concept of sacred space needed to work for me.

That morning I was struggling with my lonely "little girl" part who wanted a partner and mate again. She came up often, and that morning, I was tearful and sad. I lit my candle and while feeling it's warmth and glow, I brought my special childhood charm bracelet to my heart and tried to feel the sorrow of this "little girl" part. It was deep. I grabbed a purple scarf that represented the intuitive power I felt rushing up inside me.

How was I ever going to find a new partner? The "little girl" part and other parts began to speak, and I listened attentively. *How can I put myself out there again? Bringing another man into my son's life is scary.* As I listened, I felt my greater Self holding them, and I leaned into the sense of support I was giving myself. I was working hard to learn how to do a relationship differently. I tried online dating for a while, but just doing the personal profile and trying to trust the process was really hard. How could you tell if someone was just saying what they thought you wanted to hear instead of telling the truth? Fortunately, my larger Self was helping me see that I was ready to meet the right person for me. It was time.

After many dead-end coffee dates and email exchanges, I met Brett online two years after my mom's illness and recovery. Julian was doing better in seventh grade at his private school, so I had some reprieve to feel a little more hopeful about dating. What I didn't know was that the new relationship would trigger many complex feelings from my nineteen-year marriage to Peter that I hadn't yet faced. It took all my tools to figure out what was happening and how to cope with it.

Brett seemed to offer so much of what I was looking for: He wanted to build a stepfamily with his son and us. He was an outdoor adventurer, an artist, and an entrepreneur. He was experienced with teens. And he was both spiritually aligned and emotionally available. I fell in love overnight, but I was still cautious. He, too, had been through the trauma of divorce and post-divorce conflict, but he said he had done his own healing work. He offered an openness to work together on healing our families by starting a new life together. He also seemed to value my work as a family therapist and my insights on parenting.

His son Alex, who was seven years younger than Julian, was a bonus. I had always wanted to have another child. Alex lived full-time in Gunnison with his mom, but Brett had him every other weekend at his Lafayette home, and hopefully, he would have him more as he got older. Stepparenting became my special job. I read him stories and put him to bed at night when he

visited—things I had loved when Julian was his age. I moved in
with Brett, and Julian rode his bike to his private school, which
was closer, thanks to the move. That freed us from transporta-
tion issues. I turned my home into a rental, and we began to
create our new family together.

One spring evening when we were making dinner together
in the kitchen, I looked out the kitchen window at Julian, who
was jumping on the huge rectangular trampoline we had pur-
chased from my friend Carla. He seemed to be happy in our new
home. Then I looked at Brett, who was creatively adorning his
vegetarian Thai curry dish at the stove with final spicing. The
stove was covered with spices, and the counter was strewn with
leftover veggies, spilled spices, and condiments, like a well-used
artist's pallet.

"Wow that looks divine," I said. "You're such an excellent
cook, my dear."

"Cooking is an art!" he replied, smiling as he looked up at
me.

But I was noticing the feelings that were swelling up inside
me and wondered what they were about. I used my new mindfulness skills to pay attention more closely as I finished setting
the table and pouring water into glasses. I felt a huge surge of a
heaviness in my chest, and as I kept my attention on it, it
moved up, making my eyes tear up and creating a catch in my
throat. It felt like grief, which confused me because I was so
happy.

"Brett, I'm going out to get Julian," I managed to say. "Don't
serve just yet. Okay?"

He nodded, and as I went out, Julian smiled up at me as he
jumped high and then did a front roll, landing on the edge of
the trampoline feetfirst. "Did you learn that in gymnastics this
week?" I asked. "That was amazing!" I couldn't believe how fast

his body soaked up gymnastic moves. "Dinner is ready. We can watch you after we eat, okay?"

Julian had been taking gymnastics on and off for several years, but he had just gotten into it over the past few months. It was another body sensory activity that helped him manage his intensity and sensory overload. He was very athletic, and he really loved it.

"Oh, Mom, I just got warmed up. Watch this," he said before making another high jump.

My heart caught in my chest, and then more intense feelings started rising up to meet the ones already there. The new feelings were about my guilt that Julian had to endure the divorce and my concern about whether I was doing enough for him. I decided to take some private time after dinner to process more of what was going on inside me.

Then I refocused my attention on Julian, who was attempting another gymnastics trick. That one didn't fully materialize. He jumped up even higher, flipped backwards, landed on his side, and bounced onto his feet on the ground below.

I gulped loudly.

"Okay. I guess I can stop for now," he said as he walked toward the house.

"What was that called?" I asked, as I walked after him, taking conscious breaths to calm myself.

"A messed up backflip. I can do it better later," he said, smiling as he stepped into the house, headed to the table, and slid into his seat.

Brett asked him to wash up as he plated the food, and Julian quietly complied before returning to the table. I decided to leave the parenting up to Brett as I went to the bathroom and wiped my eyes. I needed a moment, and it was nice to be able to take it for myself with Brett now in the picture. I loved how much calmer I was with a partner to help me with Julian. And I felt much more confident about myself and my life. Slowly, I was getting more confident about my parenting. Julian was feeling loved and cared for by Brett. He seemed to be really thriving, and that was helping everything.

When I returned to the table, we all took hands and bowed our heads, and Brett said a few words of blessing before we started to eat. I liked Brett's leadership and strength, and having allowed my feelings to come up had relaxed me.

"Mom, you and Brett need to see me do my backflip after dinner."

Brett was eager to engage. "I think you should show me how you do it, Julian. Maybe I can learn it from you."

"I'd love to try it too," I added, "but I'm scared to jump that high." I wanted to encourage his talent, but my fear was really up.

We all went out after dinner and jumped on the trampoline with Julian. Brett and I tried to learn his backflip and failed miserably while he executed another one perfectly. He loved it. Then he and Brett came in and watched some TV while I went upstairs to my sacred space.

As I sat down at my journal to write, tears started welling up again. So many feelings were rising up that I just tried to name them: sadness; missing Peter; loving Brett; longing for the family I finally had; missing the feeling of support from others that I was getting from Brett; feeling good and bad at the same time. There was so much there, no wonder I was feeling emotional. It really helped just to notice it. As I settled myself in the breathing meditation I had learned, I noticed the layers of emotions beginning to settle. The more I focused on my breath, the more my mind settled down and stopped trying to figure things out, and I could focus on the sensations of the emotions floating through my body.

Pictures flashed inside, like memories showing me what I needed to see: of being with Peter and my feelings of being so stifled that I'd been unable to breathe or feel myself. Peter hadn't been able to accept me as a therapist and mother. He'd shut me out emotionally, and I could feel the pain of it in my gut.

There were more pictures: of how much Peter and I had divined the dream of a life together, of being so active in the outdoors. But there had been no room for a child in that dream for him. Having a child had been my dream, not his, and I could see that now. I always wanted to be a mom and move my life forward into a family. I was now in that family, and it could be my dream come true. Yet I was grieving the life I had emerged from.

"Is this how grief works?" I wrote in my journal. "I feel sadness in the midst of happiness. My heart is now opened up by new love, so I can allow the pain of the past to bubble up and be noticed." I decided to learn more about grief work and explore more about what had allowed the opening I'd just experienced. I thought I had already worked through what had happened with Peter, but I was learning about the depths of love and grief and how closely connected they were. Somehow, my newly opened up heart space could release more of what it had been hiding or unable to process until then.

Building our garden together, literally, was one dynamic way Brett and I actively worked together to create our new life. Building brick-inlaid submerged garden beds together, mortaring and setting each brick in its place, was an example of our commitment to one another. I felt met and understood in some ways that were so deep, they drove my commitment to him even deeper. That deep settling in my life was wonderful for providing a healing container for me—another mooring, a foundation from which to grow again.

From my IFS therapy, I was learning that several of my parts didn't feel they had received enough attention and understanding from my parents. And Peter had been able to meet the needs of those unmet parts—until he rejected me. His rejection had hurt me deeply, making a deeper wound (an attachment reinjury). At that point in the new relationship, I had dropped into a very beautiful place of healing and rejuvenation. With new tools, I was learning to listen to what needed to unfold inside me. Mindfulness gave me the ability to listen to and witness my parts. IFS gave me a road map. It also gave me an awareness of the value of compassion and how essential it was to help the parts feel attended to and understood. I just didn't know how to generate that compassion inside me yet.

I loved where I was. We were working very well together in creating what Julian desperately needed—a united parental front. Peter and Julian stopped having visits when Brett and I moved in together, and I was worried about how that was affecting Julian. But as he was moving into eighth grade, Julian was meeting and hanging out more with kids from his school and our new neighborhood who were rebellious and angry. They were acting out their own family pain from divorce. I was concerned that Julian might become more like them by hanging out with them. He certainly had reasons to be angry, just like some of his peers. I felt he needed more fatherly attention and strength at that important teenage time, but he also needed consistency in our parenting at home, which we were really working on.

As prescribed by many family therapists, we had family meetings. They were a way to get everyone involved in openly sharing their feelings with each other. That was the goal, but with teenagers and preteens, that was often a struggle. So we just did the best we could. When Alex visited on the alternate weekends, we did a really good job of holding our family meetings around the table after dinner. When Alex was away, Brett and I tried to set a routine with Julian for those meetings.

What we found was a lot of ambivalence in all of us. Fear, distrust, and deep pain from past losses in all three of us was impacting our ability to talk openly with each other, even though we tried. Brett and I decided to engage a family therapist to help the three of us talk through things more openly. Julian was very resistant, but he came once or twice. I totally understood his resistance. Starting over with a new dad when your real dad was invisible and unavailable was too much to talk about.

So we gave him as much love as we could. We helped him with his music and learning how to play drums more effectively. We supported his band rehearsals and the kids he was playing with. And we tried to do what I had learned was authoritative parenting: giving kids high and clear expectations while being sensitive and responsive to their needs, reinforcing positive behavior, and reasoning with them rather than punishing them.

The greatest gift of the new relationship was the support and reprieve from full-time parenting so I could pursue the tools of mindfulness and Internal Family Systems that were helping me grow personally and professionally. In 2006, I had just completed my Level I IFS training in Boulder and wanted to attend the national IFS conference in Chicago. Brett made me so happy by taking Julian (who was fourteen), one of Julian's friends, and Alex (who was seven) camping in the southern Colorado high country for the week I was gone. Even though I wanted to be with them, I felt Brett's outdoor and parenting skills with both boys were excellent, and I felt comfortable with the plan. That kind of give-and-take, the sharing of parenting and career, was what I had wanted. It was a good test of whether we were going to make it together as a family in the future.

At my request, Julian, Brett, and I went backpacking in the Indian Peaks Wilderness over a long weekend after school started. We brought the dog and the fishing poles, and we navigated our way together. We hiked into Thunder Lake, a beautiful place at the edge of Rocky Mountain National Park. It was Friday, and we'd left after work, so I was really tired. Julian was behind me, slowing down as I pushed a bit to keep up with Brett, who had walked ahead looking for a campsite. We arrived at dusk, and we still needed to put up our tent and cook dinner. I was glad Brett was there to help.

I leaned over to Julian, who seemed pretty beat, and asked if he would help Brett with the tent while I started dinner.

Brett pulled gear out of his pack and came over to us from the spot he had selected for our campsite. "Donna, no need to worry. I got this. We can do it together. Come on. Let's all put the tent up."

Julian looked up with a smile on his face. "Yeah, what about my tent?"

Brett smiled patiently, winking at me in the process. "Why don't we put up both tents together? That's more fun, isn't it?"

"Well, I really want to put up mine by myself," Julian replied. He had been camping a lot in Scouts and knew how to put up a tent on his own, and he looked for a spot to pitch his tent. Millie, our new, young Australian Shepherd, was sitting and watching Julian, and when Julian got his tent up, he let her inside to sit. But she was eager for a walk and made it very clear by her inability to settle there. Julian started to pet her. "Mom, Millie is going to sleep in my tent, okay?"

"Okay, that sounds like a plan, Julian," I replied. "We'll put our tent up by ourselves just fine, but since yours is done, please take Millie for a short walk."

Brett threw down the ground cloth, started putting the aluminum poles together that held the tent up, and handed me the end to put in the slot on the bottom of the tent edge. He popped the other side of the pole in the slot on his end and with a *whoosh*, the tent went up. Then we jointly added the second pole and it was done. I'd forgotten how easy it was with two people because I had been putting up the tent by myself for many years.

As I threw my sleeping bag in the tent and then unloaded my stove and food, I began to feel some emotions coming up again, like a warm welling in my throat and chest. I sat down on a rock for a moment. Was it love? It was nice to have a partner again who loved camping and being in the outdoors.

Brett came over to me at that moment. "Let me get the stove started, Donna. Do you want some tea or soup first? Might help us all a bit."

He got water from the stream and heated it to boiling, and in no time, Brett had a nice cup of hot soup for me. It was getting a bit nippy with the sun going down, and I took it gratefully before reaching for my jacket, gloves, and hat.

Soon we had our pot of risotto and veggies cooked and eaten. Some after dinner tea was brewing, and Julian dug in his pack for the brownies we had brought for dessert. He handed me one, and I passed it to Brett.

"Do you want to go fishing with me tomorrow, Julian?" Brett asked as he took another brownie and popped it into his mouth.

"For trout? Do you think we can actually catch one?" Julian asked as he leaned over his gear to see where his fishing pole was. "Here's my pole, but don't we need some bait?"

"I thought you might like a fly-fishing lesson. We use all kinds of flies and stuff. Remember when I took Alex fly-fishing on our trip to Gunnison?"

Julian stood up, excited. "Oh, yeah. Okay, I'll give it a try, but can you catch us a trout for dinner?"

"I'll do my best, Julian. Those trout are really smart."

I headed off to bed feeling happy and grateful. I had a man in my life who loved the outdoors, loved me, and loved my son.

The next day I awakened at sunrise with Brett, and he shot a photo of the sun rising over the mountains. Then I watched the guys fly-fishing, falling over logs, running after the dog, falling in the lake, painting and sketching, and getting sunburns. But mostly, I just kept feeling happy and grateful for my new life with a wonderful man, making a new family together.

Later, as we were taking down the tent while Julian was playing with Millie, I turned to Brett with a full heart. "I'm so happy with you on this camping trip. I love that you like to be in nature like me. I love how you want to build a happy family this way. Will you marry me?" I looked up into his brown eyes underneath his red ball cap as I grabbed his hands and pulled him to me.

Brett seemed a bit surprised by my proposal, but he hugged me back playfully and said, "Hmm. I'll think it over for a moment." He turned and finished packing the tent into its stuff sack, which he'd been doing before I grabbed him. Then he turned back to me and dropped his backpack at my feet, winking slyly. His eyes were sparkling with something that looked like playful joy, and he looked directly into mine. "Yes, I think that is a splendid idea, my dear! Let's tie the knot. I hope I'm as ready as you are." He hugged and kissed me thoroughly.

My parts were so clear that day. I had met someone who held all the qualities and skills I thought I needed to have a happy family life with them and Julian. But most importantly, Brett knew how to have fun backpacking, camping, and being in nature as much as I did. I was ready to make a full commitment if all those parts could come together in our relationship. It had taken some time for my parts to get that clarity. I had learned how to listen to all of them patiently until they felt I was present to them and cared for each of them. It was a process called "self-leadership" in the IFS model.

When Brett and I came back from that trip, we started planning the wedding for that next spring. It had to be May, when Alex was visiting after his school was out. But several issues began to arise about how to include my family. Who would actually come to Colorado for this wedding?

When I married Peter, my mother had wanted me to have it in Florida, and I refused. We had a battle of wills between us because she felt that planning the wedding was her domain. And when she came out to Steamboat Springs for that wedding in 1981, I was uncomfortable with the degree to which she wanted to intrude. I had felt pushed aside and not listened to.

But even worse, on my birthday, the night before my wedding, she questioned me about my choice of Peter as a husband. "Are you sure you want to marry this man?" she asked.

I was livid, and I stayed angry until she left town after the wedding.

I was afraid she might do the same thing again. But I had changed since the first marriage, and among other things, I was much more aware of my parts and how to work with them. The wedding would be a chance for healing things with my mom, I thought, because I could comfort my young part now—the part I called my "little girl"—and give her the love she didn't get from my mom. I could allow my mom to tell me how she felt without her feelings blocking my decision. It was self-leadership, but it also felt like inner connectedness and peacefulness. And my young parts also had Brett's love.

After talking with my mom on the phone and thinking through the logistics of flying her to Colorado versus driving, I felt the challenges were too big. Being in a wheelchair and having a frail cardiovascular system made it unsafe for her to be at Colorado's altitude, much less fly. I brought it up with Brett one Sunday morning in our bedroom.

"I need to talk about the wedding and my mom. I'm conflicted about trusting my mom for many reasons, but mostly for how she treated me at my wedding to Peter. Part of me is afraid she'll try to take over my wedding again. You know how I told you . . ."

He nodded. "Yes, I know all that, but what do you want now?"

"I don't know. I'm confused with all these emotions coming up." I moved from facing him to walking over to my sacred space corner of the room. I put my hand on my heart to settle myself and took a couple of deep belly breaths.

"She can't do anything to interfere now, Donna. She's in a wheelchair. We just need to honor and love her." He paused for a few moments before continuing. "I've lost my mom and dad, and I can tell you, it teaches you to appreciate them. You honored your dad by visiting him before he died. How can we honor your mom now?"

He was talking about the trip we'd taken to Florida for him to meet my parents a couple of years earlier. My dad was really going downhill and having so much pain, he couldn't walk. Mom was in her wheelchair. Brett had the idea of putting them both in wheelchairs and pushing them around Cypress Gardens, a beautiful natural attraction along the cypress-lined lake in Winter Haven, where they had famous water ski shows. I'd been there many times growing up and cherished the place. We brought a picnic and stopped to watch the ski show. It had been such a beautiful way to enjoy the time with them outdoors. I'd been grateful to Brett for bringing us all together in such a joyful and fun way.

He had also encouraged me to go back and spend a long weekend with my dad later that year, and I'd gone the month before he died. That weekend, my dad and I said good-bye to each other. It had been a special time for the two of us, and it was something I cherished.

Brett's words and my breathing helped me get back into my adult place of feeling self-leadership and clarity. "Yes, you're right. I now see that I feel compassion for her inability to get here. She really loves weddings."

The previous day, I'd told Brett that her doctors did not want her to fly, fearing another stroke. "So why don't we make plans to visit her later this year after the wedding," he suggested. "We can meet somewhere she can drive to and make a special weekend of it with her."

It was a great idea and a great solution. I walked over to him and kissed him gently.

"I suggest we invite all your siblings to the wedding, and I hope we get a full house," he said. He knew I was worried that few family members would attend our wedding because my brother's daughter was also planning a wedding that spring.

"I know the other wedding will keep some away, but I have five siblings, so we'll see who chooses to come," I replied.

"Well, I hope we get them all here. I look forward to getting to know them more. I didn't get to talk much to anyone at your dad's funeral."

The solution to the wedding dilemma brought my parts to a great calming place inside me. Holding them all in self-leadership, listening to their concerns, and bringing in Brett's parts all helped me make the right decision.

The wedding was a joyful event that beautiful Memorial Day weekend. My sister, Martha, her husband, and her daughter came. So did my brother, Quentin, and his wife, as well as special friends. Julian and Alex had parts in the wedding, which we held at our local United Church of Christ. We went to

Kauai for a family honeymoon trip in August that summer, and Julian and I got to redo some of our previous Kauai experiences with our new family.

That fall, Brett and I flew to a small town near Asheville, North Carolina, during the peak of the autumn colors and enjoyed a special weekend in a rented cabin with my mom and her caregiver. We had a delightful visit that included talking about the wedding with her, sharing pictures, and driving through the mountains together. It felt good to have created a safe visit with my mom that allowed me to honor her and love her without feeling conflicted by anything from the past.

She was thrilled with the fall colors and the rental house we found to stay in, and she seemed to deeply treasure each day of our adventure together. While she had not really enjoyed Peter, my mom seemed to enjoy my new husband, and that allowed my parts to feel alive and seen. I felt great joy and healing. We had some special talks and moments together that opened up my heart. Brett had navigated some powerful territory with me, and I was so grateful.

When we returned from our North Carolina trip, I was pulled back to reality by Julian's behavior at school. He was now in high school and in a rock band, and he and his band members were challenging some teachers pretty badly. The good news was that he was excelling in his drum lessons and was asked to join the school jazz band. He'd been playing percussion in regular band class, and his band teacher saw his abilities. We kept massaging the positive and not getting too excited about the negative, hoping to help him visualize his potential.

It seemed to be working, not necessarily on the grades front, but in the social and emotional growth. He was making huge progress.

I felt I had been too.

Chapter Ten

Finding Joy Within

MY NEW LIFE WITH BRETT allowed me the freedom to expand my mindfulness toolbox more, and I took the opportunity to attend that weeklong mindfulness-based stress reduction retreat for therapists at Mt. Madonna in southern California.

The retreat center was also a yogi ashram set in the beautiful hills of coastal California. I learned that the center had hosted these retreats for several years, and they attracted all kinds of people coming to learn mindfulness from Jon Kabat-Zinn, the founder of the MBSR program. The program was revolutionary because the eight-week course taught mindfulness practices in a secular way for people in medical settings where patients didn't seem to make progress with chronic illnesses and pain. It helped those patients heal when other medical interventions weren't helping. That had been the first application of those Eastern practices in a Western medicine setting.

Over many years and at least three or four books later, Jon Kabat-Zinn had created the Center for Mindfulness at the University of Massachusetts Medical School. He was a researcher, not a clinician, but he found a wonderful teaching partner in Saki Santorelli, a clinician who became the medical director, and off they went, disseminating MBSR tools to the world. I was dying for the opportunity to learn from both of them.

✧ ✧ ✧

Walking slowly in the brisk morning air, I focused on my right foot, pressing the ball of it on the concrete and then rolling the whole foot down until I felt the heel connect. I tried to exhale fully and feel my body in this flowing walking practice. Soon my left foot was already down in front of me in the next step. I had missed noticing that leg's lifting.

"Just keep moving and trying to stay present to all the sensations" were the instructions Jon had given us, but there were so many sensations with each move and shift of my body that I was overloaded by them. I brought my focus back to my hands clasped in front of my body and my breath to settle myself. That helped me come back to focusing on my feet again.

As I lifted my right leg again, I noticed I was coming to the end of my path, and there was another person coming toward me. Since we were in what was called "Noble Silence," I looked down and slowed as he passed me. Then I tried to focus on my feet again, initiating each step from the hip and tottering off-balance until I could get the toe down and then the heel, ready to stabilize before I shifted to the other side. I decided to let my breath relax to whatever it was naturally and focus on my feet, per Jon's instructions for this mindful walking practice.

Periodically, I lifted my head up and peeked at the full view of all 150 or so of us therapists and doctors at the retreat, mindfully walking on the steps and the grounds of the retreat center. The sun had come out more, and even though it was 9:30 a.m., it was still chilly. I was glad I had my gloves on. I loved that we got to do walking practice outside because my parts needed fresh air.

My body was tuning in to something it was registering, but I wasn't quite sure what it was. I had felt it deep in my belly earlier in the sitting practice that Jon led, and now it was a sense of solidity in my core as I walked. I was curious about the feeling.

A loud, sharp bell rang three times to alert us to come inside for our next practice. I moved slowly over to the stairs and followed others walking into the retreat center. I took off my hat, glasses, and coat and waited my turn to hang everything on my hanger in the closet in silence, trying not to look at the others. This was my first silent retreat, and I was learning how to navigate through the different transitions in silence and without making eye contact with others, even though I wanted eye contact. I was excited to be there, and I wanted to get to know the others. I was especially curious about the Chinese woman who was sleeping next to me on her cushion and air mattress. She was still jet-lagged, but she was in every session anyway, sleeping on her air mattress. No one seemed to care. I vowed to introduce myself when we could talk again. In the meantime, I just loved her with my eyes.

Jon welcomed us back, sat down on his cushion next to Saki, and turned to Saki, who would lead us in the next practice.

"I'd like to guide you now in a lying down practice we call the Body Scan. Please find a space where you can lie down on your back, placing the back of your head on the mat or floor and resting quietly there. You can place any supports you need under your knees to allow yourself to lie comfortably. Now begin to focus on the rise and fall of your breathing."

He joined us in lying down, which totally amazed me. He was going to actually do the full exercise as he was guiding it. I had never seen this done before. He moved the microphone over to his face near his mouth and stretched out on his back, lifting his head to talk. I was impressed! Then I put my head down and started to focus on the sensations in my body and my breath. "Begin to bring your attention, now, to the sensations in your right foot, noticing any sensations there: hot or cold, tingling or solid." He paused to give us time to do that before continuing. "Just allowing yourself to feel whatever is there without judgment, allowing it to be exactly as it is without having to do anything about it. Just noticing."

I followed his lead.

"Now, moving onto the heel of the right foot and the bottom of the foot, breathing deeply down into the foot, feeling all of the sensations that may be arising there."

He continued on to the ankle, shin, and knee of the right side, and the next thing I heard was him asking us to bring our awareness to the fingers of our right hand. I realized I had drifted off and was frustrated with myself, so I decided to try harder to stay focused. I began to drop deeper into my body, which was what Body Scan was designed to do, and I explored what was there more thoroughly.

"Bring your awareness to your belly, your lungs, and your stomach and to the organs in this region of your body. What do you notice there? Notice the ribs and how they are holding it all together so nicely. As you breathe slowly, stay with the sensations you are noticing there in your belly."

As Saki guided us, I was mesmerized by the relaxing and soothing sound of his voice, and I relaxed more deeply as I scanned my stomach and heart area. There was a sort of energy there, and I wondered if it would settle down more. But I let go of that thought and just tried to stay present to the energy and be curious about it.

"Moving on now to your upper body, your shoulders and the part of your body that is touching the floor."

My shoulders were trying to relax as I noticed my heart pumping and my spine trying to settle on my yoga mat. It was a hard floor, but I thought I was able to notice more nuances in my breath and body by being right on the floor instead of on an air mattress, which was what some of the others were using.

I dropped deeper into his words as he said, "Now become aware of your skull pressing deeply into the floor and all the sensations there."

I let go totally as his words rolled past my ears, and I must have fallen into a state of deep relaxation. I wasn't asleep, but it was heavenly. I came back to reality with the sound of the bell.

Next was another walking meditation practice, which, we were told, was also a break if any of us needed one. I silently and earnestly moved toward the door, repeating my earlier process of getting my coat, hat, and gloves from the closet and moving toward the door where I had left my hiking shoes. I took off my slippers and put on my hiking shoes. Parts of me were ready to get away from the crowd and walk more of the grounds.

I noticed an unpaved wooded trail headed up into the nearby forest area. My adventurer part was calling me on, and I consciously stepped onto the gravel path and headed into the forested area, attracted by the size of the huge trees and mysterious forest light. As soon as I got into the trees, I began skipping and whooping with delight, as if a child had taken over my body. I was so gleeful and alive with joy, I could hardly contain my intensity in that moment. I just had to let the experience unfold and follow with my body and my heart, so I ran and skipped farther through the trees until I came to a clearing where the path forked. I was unsure if I could find my way back if I took either of the paths, and I suspected my break time was almost over, so I turned around and headed back.

But I was distracted by what was bubbling up from deep in my belly. I recognized it as joy—pure, peaceful, blissful happiness. I felt that joyful part at a depth I had never felt before in such full-ness. I wanted to keep that joyful part in the forefront forever, but even as I longed for her to stay, I knew that was not possible.

I looked up at the tops of the trees, following their line of brownness until it opened up into the sky and the vast blueness all around. The trees were guiding me, and my eyes allowed the bright expansion I was feeling to carry me beyond my world, beyond the forest, and beyond the retreat center to a mystery beyond all of them. I was pulled into the vastness I felt both inside and outside me, and I allowed it to penetrate all of me, where I could feel it deeply. I took in a deep breath and felt it go down deep into my belly. Then I dropped into gratitude as I walked quickly back to the paved path and got in line to go back inside.

When I came to my usual spot on the floor, the Chinese therapist was awake, and I held out my hand to greet her. Since we were still silent, I couldn't talk to her, but I put my hands together in a bowing gesture, which I had learned was a Buddhist bow used in greetings and at other times. She bowed back, and a smile appeared on her face as she sat down. I want-ed to know about her work as a therapist in China, and hope-fully, we'd get to talk about it at the end of the week. I sat down next to her, and she placed her hand on mine briefly. I liked the warm connection we had made.

Later in the week, I was able to process and feel more of the expe-rience of intense joy and happiness. Though I hadn't seen or noticed it before, I had now somehow allowed a place for it to be inside me. I knew it was a young part of me that needed to be dis-covered fully, but it had taken the retreat setting and the practices to help me find a way to let her out. The mindfulness practices had taught me to trust myself more and allow a slower, calmer way of being with myself that created the development of inner trust and curiosity. When I was eating, walking, or sitting in silence, I began to reconnect with that part and feel her inside me more often. I realized it as my sad "little girl" (my exile) who had been burdened and pushed down for so long. Now she was free and unburdened, ready to be with me fully. I felt more whole, more solid, and more connected to all of myself.

We came out of silence the last two days of the retreat. Jon and Saki talked with us about the tools and process of teaching an eight-week MBSR course. We had learned all the tools, but now we learned about the technology of the program and how the mindfulness practices worked their alchemy so students like us could come to the awareness of deeper bodily sensations and know how to work with them.

"When we can categorize these sensations into 'pleasant,' 'unpleasant,' or 'neutral,' we can begin to tolerate them more easily and allow them to be there in the body to process," Jon explained. "Naming them allows us to accept the painful as unpleasant, and suddenly they become more neutral as they begin to shift and change—as they always do. You see, all of this is part of a constantly changing process inside us, and if we can allow ourselves to see a larger perspective, we can give ourselves over to this new awareness. In time, our minds begin to relax, and this reduces our experience of stress in the body, which is created by our thinking, thinking, thinking."

Then he showed us two diagrams that represented a person's pattern of creating stressful thoughts and how the process of mindfulness could allow that pattern to be interrupted over and over again until the stress was lessened, over time, as the pattern changed. Mindfulness could change the brain and its tendency to ruminate and focus on finding problems. That's why the program was called "stress-management." We were teaching people a permanent way to reduce stress in their lives by changing how they learned to intervene with their mind's process and shift things into the body. I could see how this was happening inside me the more I practiced mindfulness.

When I got on the plane to return home, I noticed how everything was bright and shiny and in my face. I had a new perspective that I could feel deeply, and I wondered how long it would stay with me.

Once home from the retreat, I practiced every day, studied the manual, and began to set up my own MBSR class to teach. I began to notice how mindfulness had allowed me to slow down and deeply experience parts I hadn't felt before—more than what I had been able to find with the IFS process. Maybe other clients needed the same deeper mindfulness experience to be able to do IFS work. It seemed like a prerequisite for deep inner healing because it had given me a way to stabilize and ground myself first and build self-trust. It also helped me sit with and appreciate my protective system of parts that had shut down my "little girl" parts earlier. And that allowed them to move over and let me get closer to that specific exile.

I needed a tool like MBSR to practice daily so I could learn how to settle more deeply into my body and explore those deeper parts of myself. Mindfulness had been a breakthrough for me, just as IFS had been. It was a regular path and process to help me stay calm and connected to myself and to more deeply develop the relationship with myself I needed to unravel the intensity my parts created inside me. I now had more tools for my inner journey and for finding the spiritual path I felt calling me. Somehow, I needed to go deeper into myself, and while I wasn't sure why, the path I was on felt real, authentic, and greatly healing.

With this new mooring, this deeper grounding, I was able to do more deep diving within myself. Working deeper to befriend my "little girl" gave me a sense of solidity and strength, and it greatly enhanced my family therapy practice. I could jump into areas where I hadn't been as confident before, like working with couples, which I had stopped doing after my divorce. I now felt more comfortable working with families with preteens and teenagers and with step-families.

I also began to develop new programs for women in transition, which I decided I was getting more skilled at navigating in my own life. Each transition was showing me more of who I was. My tools were growing, and I was applying them for myself and for my clients. I incorporated MBSR tools in every women's group I put together, so I was guiding women to find their own paths and their own healing through the MBSR teaching tools. That was the kind of empowerment I wanted to give women. I wanted them to have the tools to heal themselves instead of relying on someone else to heal their brokenness because healing yourself was like rebirthing. You found more of yourself beneath your previous experience and beneath the pain that you hadn't known was there before. And that discovery broke you open in ways you never imagined could happen.

That was the "New Me" I was finding, and I wanted other women to have that experience too.

Chapter Eleven

Riding the Waves of Midlife

HOW DO YOU RIDE THE WAVES OF MIDLIFE? Sometimes they are bigger than anything you've had to deal with before, and just like ocean waves, they don't stop coming. The next several years of my life, my mid-fifties, were full of constant change and challenge. My tools got me through. I used them courageously—and sometimes fearfully—hoping for the best. It was like riding a huge wave and getting washed out, then riding and getting washed out by another. And another, over and over again before I could reach the shore.

I was happy, with a new partner in a new life, and I was thriving. But I wondered if I had enough resiliency, forged from my past experiences, to ride the ongoing challenge of new waves. At seventeen, Julian was moving through high school, and I was approaching the empty nest. Brett, on the other hand, was experiencing the preteen years with Alex, who was maturing faster than his age of eleven, emotionally and physically. With my fingers crossed and the pressure on, Brett and I successfully coached Julian through major high school challenges. He was driving, dating, playing in a rock band, and growing with his music lessons and band activities. Academics were not his strong suit, but taking him to look at college music schools in his junior year helped him get more motivated so he could have a chance at college.

✧ ✧ ✧

Finally, we were sitting in the hot sun on the first row of seats at Julian's graduation in the spring of 2010. We watched members of his class walk across the stage to the podium, and then it was his turn. In cap and gown, a small smile crept onto his face and got bigger when he accepted his diploma and walked off the stage.

I turned to Brett, sitting beside me in shorts with a ball cap shading his eyes. "I can't believe this moment is happening!" I squeezed his hand. I was glad I'd worn a broad brimmed hat, but it was so hot that sweat poured down my forehead and along my ears. In a cotton skirt, flowing blouse, jewelry, and sandals, I was as dressy as I could get in the heat.

"Did you see the principal when Julian walked across the stage?" Brett asked. "He looked as amazed as us to see Julian graduating. What a great thing it is that these people have been so supportive of our kid. I'm so proud of what we've done here, Donna." Brett had tears in his eyes as he looked at me and held my hand, kissed it, and affectionately put both of our hands together on my leg.

"Yes, I'm grateful too—grateful that we got here together and that Julian received the support from his teachers to do so well in this program." I saw Julian's band teacher and waved to him as he walked past us and went to the podium to speak. He honored all the senior band members, and Julian was asked to stand up and be recognized.

Then so many feelings began to pour out of me that I just sat there and allowed myself to notice them and be curious about them. I had learned that the first place to start in moving toward feelings was to be curious, not fearful. And I wanted to feel them all and allow them to be there without being afraid of any of them. Choosing to savor them was a new experience for me.

I turned to Brett. "I'm crying inside and happy too!" I pulled out a tissue and wiped at the tears rolling down my cheeks. Brett squeezed my hand again. "We did this. We worked hard together to help him find this success. We should be happy!"

"So many moments, it's been scary. And now we're here. It's hard to believe and process. That's all." I was trying to process it, and naming it was helping. I was noticing worry leading to joy and fear leading to excitement, and I continued to note them as I talked to Brett. When we stopped talking and just sat there, feeling it all, I noticed that the task of parenting Julian and Alex together was the glue that held our relationship together.

When the ceremony was over, we congratulated Julian and took some photos, but it was clear that he wanted to go hang out with friends. It was a tiny bit painful to notice that. Then, as he walked away, I felt a huge lump in my throat and tightness in my heart. I wanted to pull him into my heart and hold him forever, and I knew I couldn't do that. Everything he and I had done together welled up within me as feelings. I was cherishing our closeness when he was younger, the strength of character blossoming in him now, and being able to feel his vulnerability behind the excitement of his achievements. It was all there. In that moment, I realized that I had to start letting go so he could find his way in the world. That was the hard part: letting go. That was what I felt in his need to pull away to be with his friends. He was giving me the message in his own way.

After the ceremony, Brett and I headed home, and it felt like a letdown. I wanted to talk to and be with friends instead of feeling so much emotion. I needed to process with people who were able and willing to hear my feelings, and I realized I wanted to talk to another woman. I thought of my neighbor, Celeste, who had become a confidant and friend. I was sure she could listen as I expressed all the feelings moving within me. Fortunately, she was home, and she was both available and willing to listen. After we talked, I felt heard, loved, and met. Brett was gardening when I returned, and I could tell he'd processed enough, so I went up to my sacred space in the bedroom to be alone with my feelings. Even though I had verbally processed them, there was something still there. Something seemed stuck. I decided to do a body scan to explore what was happening with my feelings more deeply.

As I lay down, plugging in my earphones so I could hear Jon Kabat-Zinn's guided meditation, I began to notice the intensity of the feelings flowing through me. My feet were twitching and wouldn't settle. Breathing deeply into my feet, I noticed the sensations there, and as I focused on them, they began to relax.

With more deep breaths, I noticed the tension hanging out in my upper back and shoulders as they pressed into the floor. I breathed into them, noticing the tension with curiosity. That felt grounding. And then I noticed my buttocks and upper thighs relaxing more into that floor comfort.

Getting more curious, I noticed that most of the fear and sadness was in my solar plexus and stomach areas, but my legs were trying to release them. It felt like grief. It was really helpful to feel those sensations, so I just allowed them to stay there without needing anything to change. With each body part, I slowly noticed any sensations or feelings and witnessed them.

When I was done, I was able to just lie on my back in Savasana with closed eyes and feel it all. I noticed a calmness all over me. I had released the sensations of grief through my body, and I didn't need to process it verbally. That was new for me.

✧ ✧ ✧

But days and weeks later I kept feeling more uneasiness, some-thing there underneath the grief. My body was trying to tell me that things weren't right even though Julian seemed to be on his way to college and was doing well. I began to spend more time alone processing what was there and being curious.

I recalled 2008 when we were reeling from the financial downturn. Brett's photography and publishing company had been greatly impacted, and he found himself struggling finan-cially. Since then, he'd been doing a lot of freelance work and new projects in an attempt to make more money, which kept him running and stressed. I was feeling challenged in the rela-tionship and was showing it by worrying about getting Julian launched.

I realized I had many parts that were angry and distrustful of how Brett had been treating Julian over the past four years, since his eighth grade year at Bridge School. Somehow I had slowly given up my power and let Brett take over more of the parenting of Julian. Now I was feeling guilty and overreacting to make up for it. I needed to be more self-led, to manage my parts better, but I couldn't seem to get there.

I told my therapist about a day that first year we were all liv-ing together when Brett was yelling at Julian to clean his bath-room. "I don't need him to keep his bathroom spotless, Brett," I'd said. I stood outside the bathroom and asked him to stop yelling, but he didn't, and Julian began to cry. Somehow I couldn't get my words out. I just witnessed that moment as I stood frozen and helpless to intervene for my son. Was I frozen because Brett's behavior was sometimes unexpected—just as my dad's outbursts had been? What "little girl" part stopped me from acting, triggered by that familiar male behavior? I remembered ignoring my dad's outbursts because I needed his love and warmth and held onto that part of him desperately.

By listening to those parts more deeply to explore the conflicting feelings there, I began to reexamine the past few years. I realized that Julian's acting out with the other kids in eighth grade might have been because of what had been happening at home. When Julian moved into high school, Brett managed him a lot while I was seeing more and more clients. And I let him take the lead in handling Julian's challenges with teachers, doing homework, picking him up after himself, and talking to the principal when necessary.

Julian then distanced himself from me. I didn't blame him. I had left him at his most vulnerable time, but I hadn't realized it then because I was so focused on building my practice. But more importantly, I realized I had been hiding behind a young part I started calling my "polished part" that knew how to make it all look good from the outside. I was letting her lead unconsciously. I had felt hopeless as my exiles kept reacting and freezing again, unable to take action. I knew it must have been scary and unsafe for Julian. And sadly, I was the parent. I had been lost at sea again.

I worked through it all by getting more perspective, by going to Chicago where Julian was now in college, and by simultaneously rebuilding a relationship with him away from Brett while I taught an IFS Level I training as program assistant. I flew to Chicago for eight separate weekends in 2010 and 2011. The process of going back and forth to Chicago and doing my inner healing with IFS with a supportive staff helped me get more grounded. I was able to be more present and loving to Julian when I was with him in Chicago.

Over time, I saw how much better I felt in the marriage with a healthier distance from Brett. I had been holding on too closely—or parts of me had been. Now that I was creating more space inside myself to be with all of my parts better, I felt more hopeful about being in the marriage and moving it to a healthier place. With new determination to make my marriage work, I looked for more ways to stay grounded in my body and allow my feelings to arise naturally and not let my guilt, fear, and worry spin me out so much.

I was glad Julian had gotten some distance too. Living and making a life in Chicago seemed to be healing for him.

The more I taught the MBSR tools in my psychotherapy and coaching practice with women in transitions, the more I saw how much mindfulness practices helped me deepen my self-awareness of my fears and intense feelings. But more importantly, I also noticed how my reactivity was lessened by sitting and listening deep inside. I began to practice insight meditation with different teachers in Boulder. I was learning that mindfulness practice could create changes in our body-minds and nervous systems when done over a sustained period of time, especially when the practitioner went on retreats where they were practicing with others in a powerful container.

But I was getting another benefit from the practices. Mindfulness also taught you how to be your own best friend. It was similar to how IFS helped me be curious about my different parts. The concept of friendliness toward self intrigued me. I knew I was not always internally nice to myself and wanted more help with that. I wanted to explore a multiple day silent retreat, and I had the additional incentive of needing several seven-day silent retreats to get certified as an MBSR teacher. I signed up to attend a woman's silent retreat up in the mountains near Estes Park that was scheduled for January, which was several months away. In the meantime, I did daylong meditation retreats and kept looking for regular groups to meditate with.

One day in early November, I was on my lunch break when I got a call from Sharon, my office mate and new friend. I'd been taking a walk with Millie, who was being trained to become my therapy dog and went with me to my office. Brett had called the office to let me know he'd been in a car accident, and he needed me to call him. I couldn't imagine why he hadn't just called my cell and wondered if he'd been hurt. My heart rate went up and my mind was getting ready to go into overdrive. It helped that Sharon's voice was calming and grounded. I took it into my heart and let it settle me before calling Brett.

I hung up from Sharon's call and dialed Brett's cell. He answered on the first ring, and when I asked if he was okay, he replied, "Yeah, but my car is totaled! I slid into the back of a semi on that icy stretch I was worried about on 285. I got picked up and brought to the hospital in Breck. I'm getting checked out soon."

He'd been on his way to see Alex in Gunnison and had called his ex to tell her he wasn't going to make it. He sounded almost in tears.

"Oh, sweetie, I know you really wanted to see him." He'd made the drive safely many times, and he was a safe driver. I felt a huge emotional pocket of energy growing inside me about Brett's challenge with his ex and his co-parenting of Alex. "What's happening with your car? Do you need me to come get you?"

"Yes, would you? I don't think there's anything else to do here, and I want to come home," he replied, sounding really down. "I guess I need to get my car towed too."

Sharon volunteered to drive me up to Breckenridge that afternoon to pick up Brett, and I was grateful to have the support and company. She was a true friend. Brett was waiting inside when we got to the hospital. He walked out as we parked, and I wondered how he knew it was me in Sharon's car. I stepped out and gave him a big hug and kiss. He was shaking, and when he looked up at me, I saw a different man there. He seemed to still be in a state of shock, and I was concerned. But he said he just felt numb.

We drove into Frisco and stopped for dinner. As we ate, Brett began to come back to his real self a bit more, which was a relief. The simple conversation Sharon provided helped us both adjust and attune better. Brett was still upset about not getting to see his son, but he admitted that the roads were really bad, with lots of wind on the stretch of 285 where the accident had happened. He'd made the trip many times in bad weather, but I was still surprised that he hadn't turned around, considering the conditions.

Slowly, some of the shock wore off, and by the time we got back to our home in Lafayette, he was asleep in the back seat.

The next weeks began a long process of healing for Brett, who ended up having knee issues, a slight concussion, and shoulder pain. He had hit his head and knee on impact, and the air bag that had been triggered injured his shoulder at the joint. He had slid into a semi, and another car had hit him from behind. There were also financial repercussions from the accident. He had to buy a car, and a claim was made against the driver behind him to recover damages. But much worse than either the physical or financial consequences were the emotional and psychological consequences of the accident, which Brett began to notice.

Meanwhile, I was getting clearer about my own parts and how I had abandoned Julian in Brett's presence and why. I was seeing the challenges in my marriage more clearly as I stepped back a bit and tried to let Brett struggle with his healing.

In January, I headed to Estes Park for a five-day women's silent retreat. My teacher was a woman quite a bit older than me with long grey hair pulled up into a bun.

By the last day of the retreat, after days of sitting and walking in silence, my senses were very alert. I had loved the trees, the sun, and the dirt roads we walked during our walking meditations and on breaks. But the best place had been a hillside far up from the cabins with rocks and a great view of the park. I went up there on breaks to be alone, to look at the mountain views, and to notice the impact of the retreat working its magic through my body. I found some joy and peace underneath the worry and sadness I'd brought with me to the retreat. Being in silence allowed me to become deeply curious about myself and my fears about being there for myself, about self-forgiveness, and about accepting myself just as I was—unlovable parts, lovable parts, and loving parts all together inside me. The experience of taking myself on retreat and nurturing myself was allowing feelings of self-compassion to arise naturally.

The last night of the retreat, the sunset filled the western windows of the room where our teacher waited for us, somewhat hidden in the shadows and sitting cross-legged on cushions on the floor next to an altar holding fresh flowers. The retreat Zendo was in the small living room of a rental house on a hill overlooking the town of Estes Park and Rocky Mountain National Park in the distance. Candles were burning, and I noticed lots of tissue boxes near her on the floor. I had forgotten slippers when I'd packed for the retreat, so as I filed into the room with the other women, I noticed the coldness of my feet on the floor. As we took our cushions, I felt the heaviness of lots of emotion in the dark room.

Then the teacher began to talk about *metta*, a Pali word for loving kindness practice. She had us lie down and find a position that allowed us to feel comfortable so we could allow our hearts to relax. As she played a special chant of women singing *metta* in the Pali language, I started to feel as if I were floating. My body melted in the warm and loving feeling in the room that wrapped around me and held me. I felt love coming from the teacher and floating through all of us as we all generated more and more of it in our own hearts.

The room became so hot with the intensity that I pulled off my covering and let the warmth soak in. Her words said something about bringing in love to ourselves. I was somehow ready for that because I felt a shift in my heart. It was as if my heart was opening wider and deeper to hold everything that was there: all the parts of me that needed to feel loved and accepted, all the parts of all the other women hurting, and all of the suffering beyond that room. I realized I could hold more than I ever knew I could when I first took in love for myself.

When I left the retreat the next day, I knew that something big—something profound—had happened inside me.

That winter and spring I felt refreshed and better, and Brett and I planned our family summer getaway to be a visit with Alex to Orlando and my family beach house in Vero Beach. But stepparenting issues were now becoming challenging in my marriage. It wasn't that I couldn't be engaged in the parenting of Alex. I loved being with him, and I had a special connection as his stepmom that allowed us to have fun together, like sharing our common interests in mountain biking and cross-country skiing.

But Brett wasn't free to create a life with me and Alex like he was able to do with Julian because Alex was in Gunnison, which was over two hundred miles away. And his ex was a difficult fixture in the mix because she wouldn't allow Brett to create connection and adventures with his own son without challenging him constantly.

I was feeling the heaviness about it on my walk on the beach our second morning of vacation. Brett had taken Alex, then thirteen up to Walt Disney World for the day, and I was enjoying a day by myself at the beach house.

Later, Brett and I went out after dinner to walk on the beach. The sun was setting, and it was a beautiful low tide with pink and purple clouds swirling above the waves breaking out in the distance. We strolled down about a mile and were heading back when he spoke out of the peaceful silence. "I think I need to move to Gunnison now that Alex is going into ninth grade next year. He needs me to be closer and more in his life."

I froze as I heard Brett's words and then walked a bit silently before I could form some thoughts. "What? What do you mean, move to Gunnison? We live in Lafayette and have a home there together. Are you going to move there alone?"

"We could buy something down there, and you could move your work there too. Remember, you told me that you could enjoy living in Gunnison. I need to have normal parenting time with my son."

"But why do you think he needs you to move there?"

"He needs his dad. He just does! I can't explain how it feels, but I need to be there and help him through these years." He was stomping in the water at the edge of a wave as it was going out, and his pants legs were wet up to his knees.

I stumbled as I tried to express my feelings. "I haven't heard you say it quite like this before, Brett. Can we talk about it a bit more?"

"I haven't felt it like this before—until now, being with Alex today. He needs me, Donna. He needs his father in his life more than ever now that he's in high school. I can't help him get through this time living in Lafayette. He needs me!"

I decided to just listen for a while because I had so many conflicting thoughts and feelings coming up inside me. How could he not see that moving down to Gunnison would cause more stress for Alex? I used my IFS skills to notice the different parts of Brett coming out and to bring some compassion for him. His younger and very emotional boy part was speaking, and I knew he was hurting a lot inside. I wanted to help him, but his request was unrealistic.

"We talked before about getting a place in Gunnison," he said. "I'm asking you now to help me make that happen for Alex!"

I felt pulled by the pain of his young part and jarred by another part of him—a demanding part. Of course I wanted to help Alex, but this was not the way. I had to respond with my adult part. "I don't see how that can work financially? Plus, I have a private practice in the Boulder area."

"I need you to support me right now," he said almost angrily. "I need you to do this for me."

Then he walked off down the beach. I knew that nothing I could say would help right then because there were many conflicting parts coming up for both of us. I let him go and headed back toward the house. Alex was reading in the living room, and I spoke to him before heading to the master bedroom, where I wrote for a while in my journal. I had many feelings coming up, and I needed to sort them out through journaling.

When Brett came in from the beach a while later, he was withdrawn and tired. I'd been sitting on a chair in the corner meditating before he came in, and I could see that his shoulder was hurting where he had just had surgery—the last one related to the accident—because he was holding it with his other hand. He flopped down on the bed.

"Are you with me?" he asked. "I need to know where you are," he added, pressing the issue.

When Brett used that kind of pressing tone, I often felt flustered. I needed some space before I could have the conversation with him we needed to have, and to get that, I needed to set a boundary and end the conversation for the time being. My adult part jumped in. "Brett, we've talked enough tonight."

And with that, he rolled over, got off the bed, and headed to the shower.

We never talked about moving to Gunnison again.

Chapter Twelve

Grief as a Guide

I WAS CHANGING CLOTHES after work when the message came in on my iPhone. "We're losing her," my brother, Quentin, wrote. "Mom is fading. We're all sitting here with her in her bedroom with Melissa."

Melissa, Mom's full-time caregiver, had been in the home with her since our dad had died four years earlier. Mom had never really gotten much movement back on the right side of her body after the stroke, and she'd been in a wheelchair ever since. She'd settled into a more emotionally blunted representation of herself, and I experienced it as a painful loss each time I visited her.

I immediately picked up the phone and dialed his number.

"What do you mean?" I asked when he answered his phone. "How do you know she's dying?" I began taking some conscious breaths to steady myself.

"Well, you know she went to the doctor in Orlando today—the one who was treating her bladder cancer. The nurse told Melissa that her urine was dark, like her circulation was slowing down. That is an indication of her organs starting to shut down. Since then, Melissa has been keeping us in the loop about when we should all gather and be with her. She appears to be fading now."

I wanted to be there, to see Mom's face. I wanted to know how she felt about being in the state of dying and what was going through her mind and her heart. But I couldn't ask Quentin about those things. "Who's there, Quentin? Is everyone there but me? Can I stay here by the phone, listening? What's happening now?"

"Wait. We're losing her, Donna." He stepped away from the phone, and when he returned, he said, "She's gone. She just slumped down in her recliner, and Melissa said she's gone."

I thanked Quentin for keeping me a part of the process and hung up. I wanted to ask him to call me later, but I knew he wasn't the one to give me the information I wanted.

I asked myself what I wanted in that moment, moved away from the phone, and walked to the window. I could feel a familiar panicky feeling swelling up inside me—that old familiar fear response. I named it and began mindfully breathing, focusing on my breath and following it through three cycles of inhalation and three cycles of exhalation. That worked when I couldn't leave whatever situation I was in and go to my sacred space to be alone. The breathing brought in a mindful moment, slowed down the thinking reactivity, and helped me settle into my body and feel more grounded. When I was back in the present moment, I checked into my feelings, which I knew were there but were hidden by the fear.

I wanted to be home in Florida with everyone—to be connected. And I felt an amazing awe-ful moment of many intense feelings happening at once inside me. I just allowed myself to feel as many of them as I could. I was amazingly calm about my mother's death. Finally, after I felt all my feelings, something was relieved inside me, and I was really curious about that relieved feeling.

Then I walked to the top of the stairs and called to Brett, "We just lost my mom."

Alex had just arrived for a visit, and he was making dinner in the kitchen for the three of us. We had picked him up earlier that day from his weeklong Woodward freestyle skills summer camp at Copper Mountain.

I went to the bottom of the stairs and stood there as Brett came toward me looking concerned. I was numb. "I want to call Melissa and find out what happened." He nodded. I told him I'd join them in the kitchen in a few minutes as I dialed Melissa.

When Melissa answered, it was clear that she had been crying and still was. Like family, she was already missing Mom.

"Melissa, can you talk to me about what happened today and why Mom went so fast? Did you have any warning? Did she know she was dying? Did the doctor tell you anything when you were at the office in Orlando?"

"Well, the nurse told us they could tell her organs were shutting down by the darkness of her urine," she replied. "But we didn't talk about it with her. I just took her home, hoping it wasn't going to happen too quickly. But I called your sisters and brothers and asked them to come over and be with her. I'm sorry I didn't call you then, Donna. I'm sure you wanted to be there too."

It was helping me to talk with her, and I thanked her for that. "Did you talk with her about what was going on once you got her home? Was she clear that she was close to the end? How was she handling it all when she got home from the doctor's office?"

"Your mom was so strong. She knew what was happening, and she didn't want to worry anyone. But she was glad to see everyone when they arrived."

And that was how she did it, keeping her feelings to herself and showing the strong woman image outwardly, even as she died, I mused. I thanked Melissa for her help and her love before hanging up.

Over dinner, Brett and I talked and decided that I needed to go to Florida alone for the week. His two-week visit with Alex was just beginning, and it was not possible for him to go with me. Brett and I had become distant at that point. After our Vero Beach vacation, Brett and I had not been able to talk through anything very well. A huge chasm had grown between us, and we couldn't seem to bridge it. When I tried to reach out to him and talk about things, he was brusque and resentful. I felt he was holding me hostage, as if he somehow expected me to pull him and me through the impasse we were at. He seemed entrenched in the desire to parent his son full-time. It felt like I had lost the loving husband and family man I had married. I wondered how I had gotten to that place, and I was grateful I could leave for a week.

I went into the bedroom, packed quickly, and then booked a flight to Florida that was leaving the next morning. Brett dropped me off at the bus station nearby to avoid the long drive to the airport.

On the airplane, I was glad I could get a window seat so I could go inward and meditate. I needed to get grounded and experience everything I was feeling in that moment. Closing my eyes, I tuned in to my breathing, noticing the low belly where the diaphragm tightened and pulled the breath up into my solar plexus and heart. And then lingering there, I noticed a tightness around my heart that felt like protection. *That's curious*, I thought.

Then my breath expanded into the exhalation, and I felt a nice little release of the tension in my shoulders and neck. Allowing the release to deepen, I leaned into the calm settling that happened between the exhalation and inhalation. I was feeling more connected to myself—feeling the familiar feeling I had when my body's wisdom was guiding me and all I had to do was follow it and stay present.

I was grateful I could let my body lead in that moment and that I knew it was what I needed. Following the breath, sensing and feeling what was there, I sat with all the sensations and feelings flowing up inside me and held them in the breath with my body without thinking about anything. I let go of any story about those feelings as I had learned to do, just feeling and being with the sensations. I labeled them as they came up: grief, sadness, wonder, fear, helplessness, sorrow, worry, excitement, gratitude. Then I noticed something in my throat, a tingling of sensations rising up there that I recognized as emotional release, and I let myself feel it. The sadness was back. I felt the tears dropping from my closed eyes. Before I knew it, my flight was landing.

When I arrived at the Orlando airport, I met Julian, who had flown in from Chicago, where he was a freshman in music school and luckily in between terms. We rented a car and drove to Winter Haven to Martha's house. The next morning, my sisters and I and my youngest brother, Morgan, sat down and planned the memorial service. Even though we each had ideas about what we wanted, we were able to agree on certain elements of music and speakers that resonated with what we believed expressed some of the beauty of her spirit and life. I felt really good about how we all listened to each other and worked together to create a powerful service at our home church in Winter Haven. We all took a piece or part to follow through on.

I was able to give my short speech about how my mom had influenced me by exposing me to the natural world of adventure, among other things, and how that had influenced my desire to move to Colorado for my own adventures. I noticed I felt a bit numb and nervous, so any tears or emotional sensations got shut down. I realized I was presenting the "polished me," the part I had learned to use growing up to meet my parents' need for that kind of external image.

Because I hadn't been in Winter Haven much for a long time, a lot of people wanted to see me and hug me at the church reception. More "polished me" came forth. Even though I noticed this was a part of me, I also realized she was right to come out. This was the right time and the right place for her. Even though it took a bit more energy to give myself more outwardly right then, it was how my mother would have wanted me to be. I opened up and enjoyed greeting my mother's friends and being the socially astute person I had learned how to be. I could *choose* to do it when it felt right to, which was so much better than *having* to do it all the time.

At the graveside, I offered a Rumi poem about compassionate service that expressed my mom's gifts. My sisters really liked it, and it was important to me to honor her in that way.

After the service, Julian and I drifted away from the family and close friends who had gathered at my sister's pool-patio area after lunch and looked out across the beautiful lakefront and lawn. The area was filled with huge palms and expansive oak trees with grey moss draping their branches. Beyond the neatly mowed lawn was the unmanicured and natural beach filled with reeds and grasses meeting the gentle waves rolling in. The natural beauty of the lakefront beckoned me. It was time to let nature refresh Julian and me and soothe our individual emotional loads. I had finally gotten past being numb, and many feelings were swelling up inside me.

I looked over at Julian and signaled him to follow me toward the beach. He had no words, just a knowing nod that meant *I'm with you, Mom. Let's get out of here!*

We borrowed a couple of canoes from Quentin's home next door and headed out into Eagle Lake, navigating through the weeds until we could get free to sit on the stern seat and paddle. Julian dug his paddle in and his canoe took off toward the middle of the lake, leaving me behind.

That was fine. I needed the space to process. With slow, gentle strokes, I reached my left hand to the top of my paddle, squaring off the hold that my right hand had in the middle of it, like I had learned to do years earlier at Girl Scout camp. I pulled it down evenly through the water. I loved canoeing on still water. The lake was a bit bumpy, but we were getting out to the calmer places. Two deep strokes on the right and then I switched to the other side of the canoe to correct my path, pulling long and deep there. Then I placed my paddle on the right side as a rudder to steer the canoe. As I repeated that sequence, I felt the paddling soothing my body, and as I relaxed, letting the boat glide forward, my feelings and thoughts came bursting through.

The sun was glaring, blinding me as I looked out on the lake. I couldn't see Julian, but my thoughts went to him, as well as to my mother. He was all grown up, and I was so proud of him. Mom had been able to see him grow up, and even in her diminished state in the wheelchair, she carried on her life, being a grandmother as best she could to her many grandchildren. I was grateful that she had spent so much time taking Julian fishing and going on other fun outings during the years before her stroke. She had given him so much of her love and energy, and he had great memories of her.

I reflected again on how, after losing Dad and gaining a full-time caregiver in Melissa, my mom just took the stroke in stride internally. I was amazed by the strength of her will, which was part of the "new" Mom. She never complained or spoke about her feelings because she didn't want to burden anyone. She told me that was why she wanted Melissa to care for her. She kept everything tightly inside, and it almost seemed like her condition didn't affect her. But I knew it did, even though I didn't know why I knew.

As I headed out of the sun and back toward the shore, I realized that Julian was paddling right behind me. He pulled closer and said, "Mom, I want to go across the whole lake and back, but it's getting rougher out there."

"I know," I replied. "Glad you're having fun. Let's head back now along the shore. We'll be missed soon."

Julian was more like me in ways I was just beginning to notice. He really needed solitude, physical activity, and nature as much as I did, though he was not quite old enough to name it yet.

We serenely paddled our canoes back along the shoreline enjoying the egrets hanging out in the reeds and dead tree branches, staying deep enough to keep paddling rhythmic strokes. The strokes were calming me deeply inside. In those last moments on the water, I was able to process a bit more: I believed that Melissa was Mom's gift from God to help her learn how to feel love and allow it to heal her heart. She wouldn't let her family in, but she let Melissa in. She had been such a perfectionist and so hard on herself. And I didn't remember her talking about her feelings at all.

Then, in that moment, I got in touch with a young part of myself. That part wanted to caretake my mom, to hold her and tell her she was loved. I had called Melissa after the phone call from Quentin because I badly wanted to know what Melissa knew as Mom's caretaker. I realized that I was a caretaker in relationships a lot, and my young part was still connected to taking care of Mom's emotional self. That part wasn't ready to let my mom go.

In the coming years, I would learn how to hold that part in self-compassion and help her disconnect from trying to caretake others with whom I was in a relationship. But in that moment, I was learning how to let go of caretaking Julian as he was transitioning into adulthood. I was on the path to finding my wholeness.

I stepped my foot out of the canoe and began pulling the canoe up onto the shore. Julian had already beached his and was waiting for me, seeing if I was okay. He came over, and I could feel his deeper state as well as mine. We resonated with each other. Together we pulled up my canoe alongside his and placed the paddles inside both of them next to the life jackets we hadn't touched that were lying in the center of the boats.

As we headed up to the house, I asked him if he wanted to talk. "Nope, I'm okay," he said as he moved toward the porch and his cousins there.

I was feeling alive and refreshed from our time on the lake, ready to deal with whatever was next. Nature and silence had done their magic once again, allowing me to feel and hear all of my parts as they rose and fell like waves. For as long as it took, until I could settle into a calm knowing.

That evening I found some quiet space alone and practiced mindfulness. Then I sat with my parts, especially the newly dis-covered "Little Caretaker" part. I called all my parts together into a powwow. I had learned that by sitting and holding space for all my parts, they were able to see and feel each other, which created healing and wholeness inside. They could feel me lov-ing all of them, including the new one. I invited the caretaker part to join the others and to share more of how she was feeling about being discovered.

That night I began what would become a deep understand-ing of this young, brave part of me.

Chapter Thirteen

Building My
Self-Compassion Container

WHEN I GOT BACK TO COLORADO, I felt really different. I was unable to settle back into my marriage. I needed to get away. Instead of spending a week of vacation with Brett at my family beach house in Vero Beach, Florida, as planned, I told him I was going alone. He knew I was struggling with our relationship, but he didn't offer any solutions. So I found a new couples therapist in April, and we went to a three-hour-long intensive together. I learned more about myself through the process, but I saw that Brett responded differently than me. I was disappointed that the process didn't bring us closer or help us talk better. There was no impact from the session. I wasn't sure if he wanted to work on the relationship, and I wondered what was happening to him. As was my pattern, I needed to be alone to better understand what I was feeling.

I rented a car at the Orlando airport, drove the two hours to Vero Beach, and stopped at a store for provisions. It was hot there, and I turned on the AC when I got back in my car. Driving to the beach area, I almost missed a turn because I was distracted by the familiar smells and feelings that being back in Vero was evoking inside me after having been there so many times in my childhood with my family.

Later, after sitting in meditation for several hours on the deck and going back inside, I looked out the window at the rippling waves of the Atlantic in front of the beach house. The bright light given off by the rising full moon was uncloaking the mystery of the water and the night. I had never before seen the moon so bright there. I looked around, as if expecting to see someone with whom I could share that gorgeous sight, and then remembered I was alone and could do whatever I wanted with my evening. I asked myself what my heart desired. Following my longings felt like being kind to myself.

May I be happy, may I be peaceful, may I be healthy, may I live with ease were the *metta* phrases I had written down to repeat to myself after learning the *metta* at a retreat. I felt them resonating inside my ears and my heart. I deserved to be happy. I was a good person. I could be kind to myself. I had been using those phrases whenever I was struggling and needed to lift myself up with goodness.

As I watched the waves on that bright, moonlit night, my mind ran through the many things I'd come there to ponder. Should I stay in my marriage or leave it? I tried to push that question aside, stop the thinking, and just be in the moment and see what came up in my body. I'd given myself the private retreat in Florida to let everything sift and sort through my mind and body. My uneasiness gripped my stomach with an intensity that equaled the moon's brightness, and I was moved to open the door. The moonlight lured me onward, and I followed.

I remembered that it was turtle season, and the full moon was also beckoning the baby turtles to leave their safe nests and move toward the ocean. I grabbed a flashlight by the door, wondering if the full moon provided enough light to see the turtles leaving the nests. Shuffling my feet in the warm sand, I walked down the beach, twisting and tossing the sand all over my feet as a way to connect more deeply to the sensual feeling coming into my body from the damp, warm sand. It was comforting, and I savored the yummy, familiar feeling of the texture of the grains on the bottoms of my feet.

As I walked, thoughts of the familiar interior debate about my marriage bubbled up again. I felt depressed, disrespected, and unloved. In the few years since his accident, I had mostly dropped into the old pattern of abandoning myself to support Brett emotionally and help him find solutions to his issues so I could feel my marriage was still intact. But now something different was happening inside me. I was not abandoning myself. I was digging in, looking deeper at what I needed, and choosing to meet those needs.

Through my meditation practice and the retreats I'd taken, I was feeling stronger about standing up for myself, and I could see what I needed to do to not be depressed. I could choose to change how I responded to events. By bringing in kindness instead of self-criticism, I was no longer feeding my depression loop, the cyclical pattern into depression that got triggered when I criticized myself. It felt good to notice my new awareness about handling depression. *May I be happy. May I be peaceful.* I was able to feel and be with my stronger Self and not get stuck in the depressed part. *May I be healthy.* I continued to repeat the loving kindness phrases silently to myself to keep generating more warm compassion and feel my Self-energy.

I also realized that I wanted to be with someone who cared enough to work on himself as much as I was willing to work on myself. Someone who was willing to take responsibility for his own happiness, who was curious, and who was willing to seek help to find a way to make the relationship work. The motivation to do the work, to move the marriage to a healthier place, had to be mutual and equally desired.

But as I contemplated, I felt the success of the marriage to Brett was now solely my responsibility. Why was I feeling that? Had he really given up. The only way to get to a healthier place in our marriage was for us to work on changing things between us.

I was grateful that I now understood more about creating change in my life by addressing my own healing and how that healing helped provide a new perspective.

I wondered about myself and what I needed in my life. I no longer wanted to be caught up in the old pattern of taking care of someone and trying to fix them so they could give me the love I thought I wanted and needed. It was the same pattern I'd had with my mother, and I had somehow let it happen again.

I asked myself what had now made it unworkable, and I could see the truth. The "polished part" of me was not just taking over and ignoring the pain. We no longer had the boys to raise. That had been the glue that had brought us together, and I was grateful for the good parts of it. But now that it was just the two of us, we'd fallen into an unhealthy pattern of being in chronic conflict with each other. I repeated the *metta* phrases silently again as I pressed my hands to my heart lovingly, hoping to slow down or bypass the negative thinking. Then I flashed on what had happened at the office of our financial planner the previous week.

"Why don't you listen to me on this?" he'd said. "I know you need to buy Apple stock, and a lot of it. You have the money, and yet, you're not doing this. You're so rigid when it comes to the stock market, and you don't move on things quickly enough to make the best choices. I gave you a list of all the companies you need to invest in, and you ignored it. Let me take over the decisions on this and work with our broker. I know what you need to do to make your money double in just a few years. The market is hot right now. Stop controlling this, Donna."

I felt anger in my chest as I remembered the incident. I wondered how we had gotten to that point. I sat with it for a moment and noticed that at a deeper level, I felt disappointment and sadness. Big sadness. Something changed after that talk on this same beach four years ago. We became distant from and distrustful of each other.

But mostly, I kept coming back to that familiar feeling of tightness and fear in my stomach. I recognized it better now. I again brought my hands to my heart to bring in kindness and soothing touch. Paying closer attention, I saw that fear was making me stop and question whether I should stay in the marriage. I decided to turn towards this fear. What was I afraid of? I was afraid of my retirement years coming up. I didn't want to do retirement alone, but Brett and I weren't even close to being able to fulfill the dreams I had for our retirement. I tapped into the fear in my belly and realized there was more. A second divorce felt scary and shameful. I'd sworn to myself I would never get divorced again because it was too painful and destructive. I'd sworn I wouldn't do that to my son again, but he was an adult now, and I had to make the right decision for myself. My heart was pounding and huge emotions were swelling up in my chest, making it hard for me to breathe. *May I be healthy*, I said again in my mind as I brought in more soothing touch.

Staying in the shadows of my sad younger self and her grasping for the security of connection was not an option for me anymore. In my belly, I could feel the familiar sensations of sinking down and collapsing into myself. As I looked out at the water, I began to walk faster, savoring the comforting damp sand on the bottoms of my feet again. Grounding myself back to the present moment, I continued to repeat my phrases mentally. *May I be happy. May I be peaceful. May I be healthy. May I live with ease.*

I'd sought Mother Nature and the beach house retreat because I wanted to nurture myself and learn to bring in comfort and kindness, which would help me allow my unease and discomfort to be there. Then I could investigate it through my body. I felt so much love there, and I was learning how to take in that love and allow it to heal me. I needed that time and space at the beach to get back in touch with my authentic self, which I'd found fleetingly at Mt. Madonna and on retreats. Where had she gone?

I'd gotten out of balance in my relationship with Brett. Walking on that special beach and following my heart was bringing in kindness and love to myself. I was caring for myself in a gentle and loving way instead of being critical and judgmental about my actions. The pattern I'd practiced, learned from many in my family, was to blame myself and beat myself up when something went wrong and then try to correct whatever it was. In IFS language, it was my self-critic, and I was changing that pattern right then and there.

A moment later, I noticed a turtle nest with the familiar roping around it, put there by the naturalists who sought out and identified nests on that beach. It was a key turtle nesting area on the Atlantic Ocean and was well protected.

Walking up to examine it more closely, I aimed my flashlight at it. Several two-inch baby turtles were struggling in the mounded sand of the nest. As I watched them, they climbed up through the sand that had buried them for many months and determinedly moved toward the water, where their lives would unfold. I looked for the remnants of the eggs to understand their struggle better, but they were under the sand. How did they break out of them? How did they decide it was time to go forth into that new purpose in their lives? What were the signs that guided them to break free and come to the surface? I decided to follow them with my flashlight. Then, realizing I could see them just fine without it, I turned it off. The moon was glowing brightly, and it gave the surf a silver sheen as it broke and foamed on the beach.

The baby turtles washed out of the deep, safe, dry sand at the top of the beach and into the fast flowing intensity of the waves as the tide rose to pick them up. They did not know where they were going or whether they would ever find connection with others of their kind again. And neither did I. Would I stay in the marriage? Or would I leave it, just like the baby turtles breaking through their shells?

I'd been to our iconic beach home on that beautiful, serene, and private beach many times. Single-handedly, my mother had envisioned and contracted that home when she was in her fifties so we, as a family, could enjoy the beautiful, natural, and wild setting. That special place had comforted me many times in my life. My strong values of family and home and my desire for deep human connection seeped into my heart, and I knew the beach house was the place to make the right decision about my marriage. There I was grounded in all that made me solid as a woman, a mother, and a wife. But more importantly, I had Mother Nature there to remind me what my body loved and knew about being fully alive and free. Mother Nature and that place provided the mooring I needed to make the decision.

Then, as if inspired by all of those sensations and feelings and the freed turtles showing their spirit, I began to leap over the waves coming in, and I leaped like a beautiful Lipizzaner horse, my right foot soaring up and over the waves that were sparkling and catching the moonlight. When I landed, it was graceful and balanced. The ball of my foot touched down first, and then my heel came down, kissing the sand as it landed. I felt tingling in my belly—an excitement about who I was becoming. I was freeing my spirit so it could soar.

That was it. My body had given me an answer. I was free to decide my fate. I was capable of making myself happy, living my dreams, and moving on from a marriage that had once been successful but was now stuck and dysfunctional—a marriage that did not make me feel respected and loved. I needed to continue being loving of who I was and who I was becoming so I could live my strength and my wisdom. I needed to move on to grow into the whole woman I was longing to be.

I felt braver when I returned to the beach house, and I felt empowered to move forward in my life just like the baby turtles I'd seen courageously exposing themselves as they made their way to the sea. I had witnessed such a rush of life flowing out from the sand—desperation turning into pure determination to live. At sixty-three, I was beginning to find the trailhead back to wholeness in a way I hadn't done since deciding to leave my family home in Florida and move to Colorado in 1976. Now, many years later, I would be making the same trek from one place to another to find what I needed to feel alive and whole.

I had transformed into an empowered woman who could feel her own feelings and make decisions based on working through the complex issues that were a part of her life at sixty-three. And even though I was fearful and filled with shame, I took action that year to divorce Brett, with whom I had been married for nine years and had been in relationship with for ten years. We sold our house in Lafayette, and I moved in with a woman friend from my church. Brett found a place to rent. Three months later, I found a new home to purchase in the Gunbarrel area of Boulder County. I was on my own again, and even though it was scary, I was confident I had made the right decision for me.

I'd taken the time to learn how self-compassion practices could work to open up more brightness, goodness, and hope inside myself where things had seemed dark and scary. And somehow, those practices had created a deep awakening for me. It had taken a long time to get to the place of being able to trust myself and make difficult decisions—like choosing to divorce— on my own without someone guiding me or telling me what to do. I'd needed to do it by myself without a therapist, a friend, or my mom or dad telling me what I "should" do. I'd needed to stand on my own two feet and advocate for myself, and it had given me great confidence to do that.

Chapter Fourteen

Choosing Me

NOW I WAS FREE! I was both scared to step out and do what I really wanted and driven to do so. I was mindfully leaning into the fear, and I started to notice that it was filled with excitement. I had read about that kind of fear in Tara Mohr's book, *Playing Big*, as a Hebrew word *yirah*. *Yirah* was the fear that overcame us when we felt we were on sacred ground, when we felt a calling in our heart, or when we uncovered an authentic dream for our life. It was "a mysterious sense of inner inspiration," and it was way different from what I normally associated with the word *fear*. Mohr said that what I usually thought of as fear was projected or imagined and was an overreaction triggering the primitive part of the brain and keeping us from stepping out into our lives. That sounded familiar.

I listened to my heart and meditated daily to allow the new sense of my wholeness to come forward. I was inching myself through that transition, trying to notice what was happening. What was changing was my heart. It was open and full of compassion. I had unblocked my heart by choosing to listen to what I longed for that I hadn't allowed myself to do before and by choosing compassion to come in instead of negativity. I was feeling expanded instead of grieving the loss of the relationship, and I wondered if grief would come later. Even though I wasn't sure what was happening, I rode the expansion wave to see where it would take me.

First I focused on expanding my work. I continued my self-compassion training by taking Kristin Neff's weeklong course, and later that year, I completed the week of MSC teacher training in California. When I returned, I began teaching the eight-week MSC self-compassion course and replaced my MBSR classes with them. I was amazed by how quickly women in major transitions were able to find a mooring by using self-compassion practices, just like I had.

"I see how I treat my friends better than I treat myself," Cindy said to Rebecca at one class. I'd divided the group into pairs, sitting in different parts of my home office, which was where I held my group sessions.

Rebecca looked down as she listened, and then a slight smile came over her face. "Me too!"

Julie and Emily sat in the other corner of the room, and I heard only small bits of their responses to each other, but their faces revealed deep sharing.

"So, coming back to the larger group now, I'd like to share with you some ways you can bring comfort to yourselves when you're feeling challenged or suffering. The first is to bring in Soothing Touch, another important self-compassion tool. I'd like you to close your eyes for a moment." I waited for them to settle in and close their eyes. "Now, try bringing your warm hand to your heart or another comforting place, just holding it there for a few moments," I said, pausing so they could explore that.

"Now try another position—maybe a hand to your heart and a hand on your belly or a hand cupping your chin—just taking your time to find a way to bring in comfort through this soothing touch." I paused again and looked at the women as they deepened into themselves.

"Now, the second tool is to learn the Self-Compassion Break. It's a way to bring in compassion to yourself with words along with this soothing touch. First, think of a situation that you're struggling with in your life right now. Now find where you feel this difficulty showing up in your body. Bring your hand to that place—or to your heart—as a way to bring in comfort.

"Now say to yourself, 'This is painful. I'm hurting!' This is mindfulness, or step one."

As I paused again, I saw Carol beginning to tear up. Courageously, she brought the other hand to her belly as she appeared to stay with herself more closely.

"Now, notice that you are not alone. Other women in this room are feeling their own pain and struggles. This is our common humanity, or step two. Continue to stay with what you're feeling as best you can."

I saw that Rebecca and Julie also seemed to be connecting more deeply with themselves through the exercise, as if they were giving themselves permission to care for themselves.

"Now to the final step: Bring in kindness to yourself. You deserve kindness in this moment. Whatever that feels like to you, can you allow yourselves to bring it to yourself now?"

When we finished, I opened the group for discussion about the exercise and what they had experienced, and Julie was the first to make a comment. "I have never allowed myself to notice my pain like that. That was really hard, and I felt guilty about it. I felt selfish."

I nodded in acknowledgment. "Yes, those are our typical responses as we begin to try a new way of being with ourselves like this. Did anyone else feel something like that?"

Carol spoke. "Yes. In the past, I would have responded in that critical way. But today I was able to feel more real feelings. Was that compassion for myself?" She looked up with wonder and joy on her face.

"Carol and Julie, you're both feeling self-compassion in your curiosity and caring for yourselves, however it's showing up right now," I replied. "All of you, just let it be there and feel whatever you're feeling in your heart and body right now. Each of you is feeling curiosity, and that will lead you to the capacity to care for yourself as you stay with yourself in these moments."

As the other women continued to share and explore together in this first two-hour group, I gave them a handout of the tool. "This Self-Compassion Break is a tool you can use anytime you're feeling stressed or are struggling with something—anytime you feel something painful or difficult that knocks you out of balance in your day. Just bringing in soothing touch first warms up your heart and signals your body that you need softness and kindness. As you practice, you will be able to shift how you respond to difficult situations by giving yourself comfort and kindness rather than criticism and judgment. The research shows that this allows us to be more productive and less reactive than if we're hard on ourselves when something goes wrong."

On week four of the group, we wrote our own loving kindness phrases as another tool to bring in compassion and love to ourselves. The women were instructed to say to themselves just what they longed to hear from others and to put that in a wish to themselves. For instance, *May I be kind to myself. May I be patient. May I feel my own joy.*

"These phrases can be used at any time to help you bring yourself back to caring for yourself when things feel difficult," I suggested. "Loving kindness practice is a way of bringing in goodwill to yourself, which—over time, with practice—will begin to counteract the brain's proclivity to look for problems to solve. We can simply give ourselves the gift of goodness and kindness instead."

The process of teaching the mindful self-compassion program gave me a buoyancy and lightness that I carried through my day and throughout the weeks between classes and clients. I realized how much practicing the tools was brightening up my life during a time when I was going through the uncertainty and ungroundedness of my divorce transition. I was grateful that life was offering up much for me to learn and expand into, allowing me to get a larger perspective about my experience of suffering and challenge. At the time, I didn't know that's what I was doing, but I was expanding myself intuitively by seeking those opportunities.

I also jumped into more training for my business. I took a ninety-day business coaching program to build a stronger coaching program for women in midlife. I had always wanted to follow my family's prototype of business, which was entrepreneurship. The coaching program was perfect for me because it was for women entrepreneurs, and it had been created by and was taught by a woman. It brought a sense of community and support to women in business that I had never felt before. It was very inspiring and gave me the tools and excitement to jump into developing more group programs, which helped me grow as a coach and facilitator.

But the most exciting gift I gave myself that year was training to be a yoga teacher. I put my practice on hold for five weeks and did a deep dive into two hundred hours of Anusara-based yoga training. Based on what I had learned from my experience with therapeutic yoga, aerobics, and Pilates, as well as my experience in Arielle's class two years earlier, I knew that adding training in yoga to my offerings would give me another way to support women in midlife through their bodies. At the same time, I was noticing how much each of these experiences was growing me, empowering me to be fully open and alive in every moment. I was gaining all the tools I needed to offer women's retreats in the future.

All of these events and trainings kept me connected and feeling loved, a strategy I realized I used a lot in my life when I felt unsure or alone. As an extrovert who loved to be with people, I could warm up my heart when I was lonely or sad by being with friends or even putting myself in a situation where I was meeting new people. And as I stepped into my new life of being on my own for the first time since my twenties, my strategy was to embrace what was coming forward instead of staying home and feeling my aloneness. What was coming forward was bringing me joy. I was choosing to savor it all totally—to practice more self-compassion.

Julian graduated from his music college, and I flew to Chicago, where I was joined by Martha and Joe and other family members to celebrate with him. Then my niece, Allison, got married, and we all went to North Carolina to be with her and her new family and to celebrate life's joys again. It was a huge family gathering, and I loved being with all my siblings and catching up with them. I realized how much I needed loving family connections at that time.

That spring, another remarkable thing happened. I was serving as the president of Boulder Business and Professional Women and was leading an event at which Colorado nonprofit agencies that supported women could come together to share their work with us. While visiting the organizations' booths at the event, my eye caught a sign: Climb Mt. Kilimanjaro with AfricAid. I stopped in my tracks and struck up a conversation with Maria, the executive director of AfricAid. She told me that the trip was a fundraiser for girls in Tanzania who were in their Kisa Project.

"Really? What is the Kisa Project?" I asked.

"It's a leadership training program for African girls in the last two years of secondary school. It prepares them for university. Through our programs and others, we empower them to change their lives and choose education and a career over early arranged marriages and no secondary education."

I loved what they were doing and asked about the climb.

"One of our key supporters is a gentleman from Evergreen," she said. "He's organized this trip, and he has climbed the peak many times. He wants to take five of our Kisa graduates—who are now mentors—up the mountain with us. These girls have never had an opportunity like this in their lives. This is a special opportunity to climb the peak and help our girls at the same time."

It was a great idea, and I told her I wanted to ponder it a bit and would get back to her. As I walked away from the AfricAid booth, my heart pounded with excitement and joy. I wondered if I could actually climb Kilimanjaro, and at that moment, it seemed possible.

I learned more in the upcoming weeks about how culturally groundbreaking the trip could be for those African women. They had been brought up to believe that women didn't and couldn't climb mountains. With that huge, mysterious volcanic mountain that rose to nineteen thousand feet in their backyard, they had been taught that adventure and physical endurance weren't available to them. Their bodies were for bearing children and keeping a home. Not only would the trip challenge cultural norms for the women, it would also open up huge cultural issues for the male trip leaders, guides, and porters because they had female children in their homes. Was that patriarchal culture ready to break those barriers? It would be an empowering adventure for African women. How could I not be a part of it?

In making the decision, I bypassed all my thinking parts that were filled with fear and let my body-oriented, adventure, intuitive, spiritual seeker, yoga dancer, and little girl parts decide. My heart and my adventurer part, the part that got me to Colorado in my twenties, were rising up saying that I'd always wanted to climb a big mountain and now could. My greater Self decided it was time to let the adventurer part make the decision for me. I signed up immediately and called my cousin in Durango, a great mountaineer herself, inviting her to share the experience with me. She agreed!

The trip was just what I needed to feel my strengths and intensity and feel how they could blast me into a happier place—expanding me so I could take in all of the big emotional changes that were happening inside me. I was good at physical things, strong and resilient in my body and spirit. I needed to lean on my strengths.

Deciding to go to Africa to climb Kilimanjaro was a way of saying yes to myself in a big way: Yes, I am enough. Yes, I deserve this. Yes, I can do it. Yes, I deserve to meet that longing, climb a real mountain, and explore my true strengths, both physically and emotionally.

Chapter Fifteen

Fear and Awakening

AT THAT TRANSITIONAL TIME IN MY LIFE, I began to break free from all the restraints of being a woman that I had both bought into and challenged my whole life. I had consciously created that ripe and terrifying moment in my life without really knowing why. I'd even left a marriage I never thought I would consider leaving. In spite of my pain and fear, I was ready to open myself to the path that was pulling me forward. I truly wanted to follow the path of my heart and not the path my head would have me take.

I didn't know what I was doing, but I was in touch with a deeper force inside me that was guiding me from the inside out. I was finally aware of the courage and energy I'd always used to face forward in my life but hadn't appreciated much. It had become unstoppable.

I was following that newly awakened energy as *yirah* inside me, and I was trying to look at other fears carefully so they didn't shut me down. As I climbed seven thirteeners and four-teeners in Colorado that summer and fall to prepare for my big adventure, I talked to my friends a lot about the fear I felt making the decision to journey to Africa to climb Mount Kilimanjaro. It was the first sign that I was on to something big.

All the coaching books I'd read said that when you decided to expand into something you'd always wanted to do and set that goal, the one thing you could count on was that big fear would follow. The physical and psychological challenge I had set for myself by setting out to climb a 19,425-foot mountain was no exception. That decision gave me the opportunity to really explore fear from the inside out more carefully and mindfully. I was really curious about how fear had stopped me from finding and being me all my life.

And so I journaled about it, I wrote blogs about it, and I kept trying to befriend it as best I could. As I began to notice them, the sensations of fear washed over me when I was hiking, trying to go to sleep, talking about my trip, or in session with a client. I couldn't escape that churning and exploding energy in my chest. What was I afraid of? I began to catalog my fears in my journal and discovered a number of things about myself: I feared not being enough. I had a fear of failure, of not creating a big enough life for myself. I feared letting others down and not meeting the expectations others had of me. I feared success. But I also feared not making enough money, because my dad always said, "Money is how you keep score." I feared accepting myself just as I was, because to do that, I would have to be enough.

If I was enough, I could stop trying so hard to be someone I thought I had to be to please someone else. But I didn't exactly know how to be myself. The fears seemed to be about allowing myself to be okay with who I was, and they seemed to all be fears that were projected onto me as a young girl. They had never really been mine. Tara Mohr referred to them as *pachad* fears. From an early age, they had stopped me from doing new things and exploring myself.

When I could identify *pachad* fears and move them over, so much opened up to me. I still felt fear, but I wanted to see if it was mostly *yirah*—the fear of being on sacred ground and following a calling of my heart. I would have plenty of time to explore that more. But right then, I wanted to know if I could accept the energy and strength I was feeling as positive and see that I was lovable and good without having to do anything else. Could I lean into accepting the energy that comprised me and allow myself to just be me—totally? It was my life-giving energy, and I loved it. It was a part of me I needed to embrace more. The climb would help me.

I flew from Denver to Amsterdam on the first leg of my journey. I was flying alone because I had mistakenly booked my flights a day in advance of the other Colorado folks—including my cousin. After a four-hour layover, I had an eight-hour direct flight to the Kilimanjaro airport in Tanzania. It was pitch-dark there, and I was filled with fear when I walked into the flimsy airport. Suddenly my groggy brain remembered my tour guide's message to look for a driver to greet me with a sign and a flashlight. I saw his sign as I dragged my tired self through the customs line. With great relief I read "Donna from Colorado."

I introduced myself to my driver, a man named Joseph, who said he would be taking me to my hotel. Joseph and I had a great visit on the dark, deserted drive from the airport, and I learned that he was not only my driver, he would be one of the guides. As I looked out, all I could see was the paved two-lane road narrowing into dirt and dust as we got closer to the town of Moshi, where I would be staying and meeting my group at a hotel. As I looked out at a few tall coconut palms, I smelled the tropical air, which was distinctively humid and heavy with scents. I saw very primitive buildings and dirt-floor shacks everywhere, and my heart felt the impact of how the Tanzanian people were living on the land.

It reminded me of growing up in a huge lakefront home on acres of private groves alongside the makeshift Cuban and

Mexican migrant housing communities that provided essential labor for the citrus industry in central Florida. When I was in second grade, my mom wouldn't let me bring my friend Linda home because she was from a migrant family. It was a stark lesson in how privilege was taught. I tried to stay friends with Linda as long as I could without my mom's interference.

I felt my privileged parts and tried to move them aside so I could open up totally to the African experience. I wanted a full immersion into the land and the people, and hopefully, I would feel their hearts. I was already sensing their openness and joyful outlook on life. A deeper purpose was working through me that I couldn't identify.

Because of my early arrival, that night I had to stay at a different hotel than the one the group would be at, but Joseph came by and picked me up in the morning, helped me get breakfast, and took me to the group hotel. By then I felt grateful for the extra night and day there because Joseph and I had become friends instantly. He had asked me about AfricAid and the Kisa Project and what they did, and I learned about him and his family. He'd taught his two daughters to respect their parents, as was their tradition, and he wasn't so sure about AfricAid's idea of allowing girls to choose their mates. But he did believe in education, and he wanted it for his daughters. He said that Tanzania's new president was pushing for education for all girls and boys.

When I told him about climbing up the mountain with the Kisa women, I could see him pondering it deeply. I liked his warmth and interest in our group's purpose and I liked his questions. His openness made me feel grounded and safe, and I was excited about getting a chance to know the other guides in his company.

Later that day, the rest of the group from Colorado arrived, and I had plenty of time to prepare my gear and rest. Jane arrived at noon, and we caught up over lunch. At dinner, we met Felix and his team of SENE mountain guides who would guide and lead us for the next six days on the mountain. I learned that Felix had been guiding trips on Mt. Kilimanjaro since he was ten. His company was the oldest and most experienced guiding company, and all the other guides looked up to him as a role model.

Curt, our trip leader from Evergreen, had gone up the mountain five other times with Felix. That information settled down my fear a bit. Then they showed us the map of the Machame Route, a beautiful passage up the mountain through five ecosystems, and the camps we would be staying at each night. We would start the climb at 6,000 feet and ascend to 9,950 feet the first day, about 6.6 miles. The second day, we would climb 3.5 miles to Camp Shira through the Shira Plateau to 12,620 feet. Shira cone was one of the three volcanic cones making up the whole mountain. On the third day, we would climb to 15,230 feet to Lava Tower, another volcanic area, and then descend to 13,000 feet, where we would camp that night, for a total of 4.4 miles. Then the climb would take us up the Barranco Wall, down, and around the mountain to another camp, Karanga, ending at 13,230 feet. On day five we would hike 2.4 miles up to the final base camp at Barafu at 15,360 feet.

That was the point from which all routes on the mountain completed the summit, so it would be a crowded camp. From Barafu, we would ascend eight miles in the freezing wind, starting at midnight, with a full moon guiding our steps to the base of the largest crater called Stella Point. We would reach that point around sunrise after eight hours of climbing up stair-like steps cut in the frozen lava. Fortunately, since the glaciers had receded, there would be no snow or ice on the steps. That was both sad and comforting. Then we would just have the final mile and a half to the summit at Uhuru Point, at the highest cone, Kibo.

It sounded pretty straightforward, but it was still scary. I didn't get to ask about what kind of climbing we would do on the Barranco Wall and how steep it was. I stopped listening at that point because my mind was winding up and starting to work with all the information I'd just received. Fearful thoughts flooded in, and they not only permeated my mind, they continued on through my heart and lungs, and they tightened my body. It was such a familiar feeling, but I couldn't seem to stop it even though I was noticing the fear happening. So I got up and went over to talk with the African girls going with us.

Maria stood beside Ellie, holding the gear bag as Ellie pulled out clothing from her duffel bag. I walked over to help and introduced myself.

Ellie introduced herself and then immediately looked down before peeking back up at me. "I need some help with packing."

Maria asked me to help Ellie decide on what items to bring while she helped two other women. "What questions do you have about packing, Ellie?" I asked. "You want to have enough layers, but not too many."

"I'm doing okay with my gear," she replied. "I borrowed some jackets and just need to know which one to take." She held up a puffy ski jacket and a lighter down parka. I pointed to the down parka as she pulled out some heavy socks and gloves. We sorted through them, decided on the best choices, and put the extras back in her duffel.

"So are you excited to go on this climb?" I asked.

"I really want to go, and I've done some walking to get ready, but I'm worried about going." With a sigh, she looked down, keeping her eyes aimed at the floor.

"Why are you worried?"

"I'm afraid I'll let my family down. They depend on me for my wages, and I won't be working for a week. And if anything happens to me, it could be longer." She looked up at me with sadness in her eyes.

My heart ached with her struggle. As she explained more to me, I realized that her choice to be in the Kisa program, go to college, and take a job with AfricAid meant she had to abandon the traditional role her family expected her to follow, which included accepting an arranged marriage. There was shame in the way she held herself back, and I could see the conflict inside her. Then she told me her father's reaction to her choices was to make her responsible for supporting the rest of her siblings. So all her money was going to her siblings. Her father had basically banished her as a girl and made her respond like a boy would have to in their culture. That kind of treatment felt harsh and brutal to me. Was that what Joseph had meant by respecting their parents?

Ellie and I got really connected that evening, and I was looking forward to being with her on the climb. I was a bit worried, though, about her health and stamina because she mentioned she had stomach issues from the stress of family pressure.

I also met Hadija, Elizabeth, Assinawae, and Bettina, the other four African women who would be going with us. They were all friendly, and they all had unique personal stories to tell, just like Ellie, though not as poignant. All were determined to get to the top with us. During the rest of the evening, we did trust-building exercises as a group and came up with a name for our trip: Kili for Kisa.

The next morning we arose at 7:00 and had breakfast. Then at 8:00, we loaded up into a large van that would take us and our gear to the Machame Gate, where we would start our climb. I learned a lot about the corruption in Tanzania's systems when we ended up waiting four hours at Kilimanjaro National Park before we were allowed to start our climb. Finally, we ate lunch at the Machame Gate picnic area and then started our first day's trek up through the rain forest to Shira Camp, still deeply in the trees. Our group was just learning to find a pace together, and the climb was 6.6 miles, so we arrived about 6:00 p.m.

We had slowed down and stopped a lot along the way for Ellie, who was struggling. We also experienced a two-hour rain shower that soaked most of us while the guides all pulled out their umbrellas and danced by us. That evening, I learned that Ellie was suffering from altitude sickness and had a bad stomachache. I went over to see how she was doing, and while she was in a lot of pain, she was determined to keep going.

"Do you have ulcers?" I asked. "Have you been to a doctor?

"Yes, I've had ulcers and been treated, but they aren't going away." She looked both determined and a bit lost, like she had bitten off more than she could chew. I wondered if there was more to her story, and I wondered if anyone else knew she had ulcers.

I was truly going to miss her if she stayed back. "I hope you feel stronger tomorrow and continue with us. I want you with us."

The next morning we were awakened by two of the younger guides bringing coffee to our tent, which delighted Jane and me. We lifted our upper bodies out of our warm and cozy bags to get our fingers tested with the pulse oximeter. Once they'd done that, they gave us fresh coffee.

As Jane and I dressed, we talked about the possibility of losing Ellie. Both of us were sad because we knew how badly she wanted to get to the top, and we both felt very connected to her. But as we gathered to start our hike that morning, Curt told us that Ellie had left early with Joseph to head back down the mountain. She had decided that she was too ill to continue. I was disappointed that Ellie had dropped out of the climb, but we still had Elizabeth, Hadija, Bettina, and Assinawae, and I began to focus on getting to know them.

It was overcast as we headed up through the rainforest and around the west side of the mountain, and more rain was forecast. We'd been told that looking down from that vantage point was powerful, but it was too overcast to see anything, so we just trudged through heavy brush and rushing water from swollen streams. Every once in a while, the clouds would break and I got a glimpse of the beautiful, wild, steep side of the mountain.

It started to sprinkle as we made a dangerous stream crossing. The guides supported us in an attempt to prevent us from slipping as we jumped across the rushing river. Finally, at noon, the rain poured down hard. I looked back at Jane, who was crossing the stream, and waved for her to catch up, pulling my raincoat tighter. My raincoat was drenched and worthless in the heavy rain, and I found myself wishing I had invested in more Gore-Tex.

"Maybe we should stay together. This weather is getting rough," I said. She nodded and moved up closer to me. I was feeling a bit defeated by the rain and how it was slowing down our progress up the mountain, but I knew I could keep trudging as long as I needed to.

As we kept moving in line with the group through the heavy storm, Jane wondered aloud what we would do for lunch if the rain kept up, and at the next turn in the road, a guide told us to move over to an area where they had set up the porters' tents for us. We stepped through the two inches of water on the trail and entered the tents in small groups of four or five, which was all each tent could hold. We couldn't have been more than five inches apart as we stood together, and I noticed my hair dropping water droplets on Jane's hand, which was next to mine. I shivered. Looking down, I saw that my boots were covered with water up to my ankles. Even so, instead of being worried, I was feeling grateful as I pondered how they had managed to put up the tents in the rain.

The porters and guides handed us bowls of hot soup through the open tent door flap. I brought mine to my lips and was soothed and warmed by it. Soon I felt better and was able to manage the wetness and coldness. And by then, the rain had stopped. As we finished our soup, they handed us bread and cheese, but I was warmed and ready to resume the moving meditation of ascending the mountain. That day, especially, was meditative for me. I experienced each moment with deep sensory detail as it moved through me. And as I tuned in to the sensations of my wet and damp body, warmed by the soup, I again felt open and awake for adventure. Subdued and quiet, we stepped out of the tents and followed Felix through the wet brush and muddy ground through the tree line and above it to our camp site for the night.

We were ready to go on day three, and Felix massaged our excitement until we burst forth with enough energy to make it up to Lava Tower at fifteen thousand feet, where we met the clouds again. He wanted us to push our capacity on our third day, as well as see if anyone had altitude issues. Everyone seemed to enjoy the challenge, and no issues showed up. Bettina then led the group, and the guides let her find the pace to finish our way downhill and over big rocks to our Barranco Camp at thirteen thousand feet.

Day four started with the excitement of climbing the Barranco Wall, a Class 3 rock face that wasn't really very difficult. I had climbed Class 3 on many mountains in Colorado. It was basically a walk up using hands as needed for support. But because we had four different groups climbing it at the same time, I was a bit unnerved. All the groups had shared the same campsite the previous night, and I wondered if we would all start out on the wall together that morning.

Jane and I stopped halfway up and took a break on a ledge as our porters casually strode past us, many of them carrying our gear on their backs. Other groups got intertwined with our group, and we ended up talking to some new folks, especially at the top as we celebrated our climb together. It was a tight day on the Barranco Wall.

The clouds that had been surrounding us and causing the rain for the past three days were finally dissipating. Now they just flowed in and out with the light wind. The terrain was changing, and we were getting more into a volcanic landscape that looked like a moonscape, full of volcanic rock and rocky debris. When we arrived at our camp that afternoon, the clouds had cleared, and we could see the top of the mountain. It was breathtaking, and I could not only see how far we had come but how far we still had to go.

Looking down, I saw the valley of Moshi Town below where we had started. The clouds were now beginning to cover it over. As the sky opened up to an elegant blue, there was still some sun breaking through at our elevation. We all took lots of pictures of our scenic camp, Karanga Camp, which was at 13,250 feet.

After getting settled in my tent and hanging out my wet clothes in the setting sun, I interviewed all four of the African women while Mike from AfricAid videotaped us. I was deeply touched by the passion and determination both Assinawae and Hadija had about completing their education and helping other girls just like them. They were showing that same passion and determination, along with a deep strength of character, by climbing Kilimanjaro. Neither woman had trained much for the climb except by walking as much as they could. My heart was deeply touched by their powerful presence and determination.

On day five, we only needed to climb to Barafu Camp, at 15,360 feet, from which we would make our final summit climb. Since we now could see the top of the peak, I began feeling fear again, but I was able to just notice it brewing in my belly. The more I kept hiking, the more I could keep my fear stabilized.

As we grew closer to Barafu Camp, I got more and more excited and fearful. This time I named it as *yirah*. I was able to work with it cognitively by telling myself I had trained well and was ready for the summit climb, and all I needed to do was stay with myself throughout the eight-hour climb up to the crater's rim.

We were dragging after lunch, and we could see the long line of pilgrims trudging up the steep incline above. My stomach dropped because it looked so long and hard, and it was already late in the day. Curt came over to us and said, "Now is the time to learn the rest step so you can pace yourselves up this steep path. It will be important to use this step on the final ascent tonight."

The previous night, as we sipped our yummy soup—one of the three courses we had every night for dinner in the round tent—Felix and the other guides had talked about how our final ascent was going to unfold. Even though I had already heard about the plan on the prep day, it somehow seemed scarier as they described the eight-hour trek in the freezing cold of night.

My body was trying to take it in. So learning what they called the "rest step" was another way to prepare my body mindfully. Curt started walking ahead of us, holding his trekking poles up and out so we could see his legs. Putting his right leg in front of the left, he rocked his weight from the left leg forward into the right. Then he pushed off with the left leg and brought it forward ahead of the right, higher on the trail. He moved very slowly, keeping his weight distributed evenly on both legs as he walked up the steep path. Then he brought his poles down and integrated them into the leg movement, giving more stability and support to the process.

"This hiking step helps you balance both your body and your breathing so you use less effort going up," he said while still moving forward. "And it will help you keep your focus moving forward when it becomes really steep and difficult." He turned back to us. "Now try it yourselves."

The rest step gave me the opportunity to be totally mindful in every step and be with all my feelings as they arose and fell away—to feel my fear and to keep moving through it until I got to the other side of it. Just like the walking meditations I had learned on retreats, it was a metaphor for how to focus on difficult tasks with my mind and body. It was the perfect tool for me to use on Kilimanjaro.

We left Barafu Camp at midnight after resting and eating dinner at our new campsite. The guides and porters had supported us with lots of food and with guidance about what to expect on the final ascent. They reminded us that it would be cold and windy. We would need our headlamps and all our warm gear, but a full moon would guide our way.

So we headed up Kili's summit path. Some of the path consisted of rough volcanic debris and some of it was steps carved in the molten lava. Many pilgrims had trekked up this same path before us to reach the top of the mysterious mountain in the clouds. Even though the wind was freezing, I was able to keep warm inside my ski jacket, heavy pile sweater, and warm ski mittens. My legs were layered with warm polypropylene tights covered by Gore-Tex wind pants and my gaiters over the mountaineering boots I had bought and worn in just for this peak.

We were divided into small groups, and a guide was assigned to each one. John was my group's guide. He helped me take off my gloves and drink water several times, and he helped me adjust my clothing when I needed another undershirt. I felt strong throughout the hike except for a few moments when I was freezing before I put on another shirt.

Finally, as the sun was breaking through the clouds at daybreak, we reached the point at the crater rim called Stella Point. Some of the group at the front of the line started to yell in excitement. I pushed harder past the twinges of pain in my lungs, feeling encouraged to keep moving until I got there. Soon I crossed the edge of the crater, but I knew it wasn't the top.

After resting together at some nearby rocks, Felix and the other guides joined in hugging and supporting some who were struggling with their oxygen a bit. Not only was I not struggling with the oxygen, I actually felt energized. I stepped forward and looked at Jane. She and I, along with Curt, started moving slowly with the three African women toward the path to the final summit sign, which was thirty minutes ahead. I fell in line behind them and tried to get my legs to move. It felt like they were in quicksand, and I struggled to pick them up and move them in the rest step.

Along the mile and a half to the summit, many thoughts and feelings flowed through me about my experience on Kilimanjaro with my group. But mostly, gratitude was pouring out of me as I kept putting one foot in front of the other. When we turned a corner, I could see how much farther we had to go to reach the summit sign. As I got more excited, my lungs began to tighten and I slowed to get more breath. Then I was through it, and I pressed on.

Finally, I got to the sign, where Jane, Curt, and the girls and I all collapsed together, cheering with our hands in the air. We took a bunch of pictures as Mike and the others finally joined us there. We had made it! We stood a while longer celebrating together with Hadija, Assinawae, and Bettina who had made the summit with us. Somewhere, Elizabeth had turned back.

As others headed down, I began to walk back from the sign, wandering closer to the edge to examine the melting glaciers falling over the edge of the peak. Massive glaciers had once covered the entire top of the volcanic mountain, and it had been a glacial climb to the top. But I learned that they had receded more than 85 percent since 1912, and I could hardly see them. I called Jane over, and we took pictures of ourselves in victory poses at the edge of the glaciers next to the flat trail.

Then I decided to let Jane go down by herself and walk down alone. It wasn't until I began my descent that I noticed the familiar stillness that opened up inside me when I began to hike or move in nature. But there was something more this time. The fears were gone. I felt incredible exhilaration as many huge and powerful feelings swelled up inside me, and I could feel what had been blocked by fear before. And instead of being afraid of the feelings, I invited them in with curiosity, savoring them as if they were candy. Was this rush of so many feelings the intensity that had been troublesome to my mother and passed down to be troublesome to me my whole life?

Right at that moment, our head guide came over. "How are you doing, Donna? Are you ready to go down with me?"

He and the other guides were taking us down a different way than we had come up. All of a sudden, I found myself slipping down piles of moving scree, and I was very surprised that I could somehow keep my legs moving. They felt so numb with tiredness that I feared I wouldn't be able to navigate the scree and would fall over at any moment. Seeing my exhaustion, Felix grabbed my hand and guided me through the scree. Gratefully, I followed him, unable to feel anything in my legs at that point.

Finally, after what felt like forever, we found some solid ground and began walking down a trail. My legs felt even more numb and wooden, but we got to our previous campsite and retreated into our tents. We were told that we needed to pack up our stuff and refresh ourselves in whatever way we needed to. Then we would walk down another two miles to the campground we would stay at that night.

I collapsed on my sleeping bag in the hot tent. I needed some time to be with all that was running through me and to rest a bit. I closed my eyes, but a few seconds later, Jane rushed into the tent and started packing up her stuff. She hardly spoke to me, and I realized that she was also exhausted. I had no more strength to talk than she did, and I knew I needed space, so I took my journal, crawled out of the tent, and headed for the round tent where we had taken our meals. Once there, I fell into one of the flimsy chairs at the table, propped up my legs on another chair, and drank some water. Then I began journaling. The climb had triggered a deep dive into myself, and I wanted to capture at least some of my feelings while they were still fresh.

> What I learned on this mountain today was that when I faced my fear, named it, and moved it over, I could feel a greater sense of myself—the wholeness of all my feelings and all the parts of myself being allowed to fully express themselves—and my intensity fully opened! It was finally safe to open up to all of these feelings on this mountain. Befriending my fear with courage (whether it felt like *yirah* or *pachad*) and

embracing my strengths (my energy and my physicality) was the key for me to create a safer container to feel my deeper parts I had been taught to be afraid of. Now these parts were out, and I could love them! This intensity I was now feeling was many parts all awakened and sending out sensations and feelings into my body. I was holding them all and bringing in love and compassion to them.

At that moment, John walked into the tent. "I've been looking for you, Donna. Are you okay?"

"Yes, I am. Wiped out a bit. I just needed some space alone, and I found it here. Do you need to take down this tent and pack it up?"

"Yes, but only if you are okay. Mostly I need you to get your personal stuff packed up so we can take down your tent and get it to Millennium Camp so it will be ready for you when you get there."

I appreciated his care and attention, which I'd felt from all the staff on the climb. But John and I had shared the summit together, so I felt I could respond more openly. "My body and my mind are not quite ready to keep moving. That was a big climb, wasn't it?"

He just listened and nodded with a sly smile.

"I totally appreciate your help, John. I felt your support when I was really cold up there. Somehow, I lost you and went down with Felix."

"No problem. I'm glad you made it down so well."

Somehow, I dragged myself back up to my tent alongside John, who waited patiently as I pulled myself together, changed my clothes, pulled my boots back on, and grabbed my poles to head down to Millennium Camp, two more miles down the mountain. I struggled with the aching in my feet as I walked and noticed an angry part flaring up inside me. *I don't want to push myself anymore today. I chose to be kind to myself and take a break, and I can't seem to be able to do that. I'm mad that I have to keep pushing down this mountain after all I've done to get up it. And now I have to keep going when I'm hurting?*

I sat down to see if that helped, but my feet still hurt. From my greater Self, I was able to tell the angry part that I would take care of her tomorrow. And I put together a plan to walk very slowly and compassionately down the rest of the mountain the next day, going at my own pace.

To reach Millennium Camp, we had to come back down to the tree line, and the trees almost looked like an oasis in the desert. They weren't palm trees, but they resembled them—in a Doctor Seuss sort of way. Once at camp, I found where they were putting up my tent and duffle, but Jane wasn't there, so I wandered over to where the porters and guides were starting to sing and dance to us. I began to see others from our Colorado group moving toward the music too, including Curt.

The music was rhythmic, and the African beat pulled me close, but the words were sweet and gentle. I started swaying and moving with them, totally enjoying the moment. The porters and guides leading the song pulled in Hadija to sing and dance with them. She gladly stepped up and started swaying and moving. Something really powerful had happened with the porters and guides: The men were honoring Hadija in a way they hadn't before. She had climbed their mountain, and now she was just like them. These African women had broken a cultural barrier that day, and the men were celebrating it with childhood songs, bringing them, African men and women, into a unity they had never felt until that moment on that mountain.

We watched and joined in with the dancing until it was time for dinner. Everyone was exhausted at dinner, but I could tell that the mood of the staff and guides was different. Hadija and Assinawae didn't sit together that night, as they had done the nights before. Instead, they sat next to us, as if we were now all one family united.

Felix gave us the plan for our final descent of the mountain the next day. We would go from Millennium Camp to Mweka Gate, eight miles and seven thousand vertical feet down. It had taken us five days to get to the top of the mountain, but we were going down in two days. I was concerned about how my body was going to handle it, but I kept my concerns to myself. My Colorado group was ecstatic, but they felt a bit distant to me, as if I were in a different reality.

We left the dining tent and headed to our own tents. As I lay in my sleeping bag, I noticed that something powerful was awakening inside me. The full moon rose, lighting up the landscape, and the funny trees looked like mysterious creatures in the night. My imagination was running wild, and stimulated by the magic of the mountain, I reviewed the day in my mind. I tried to hang on and listen to my feelings until I fell deeply into a restful sleep I totally deserved.

Chapter Sixteen

Answering the Call to Authenticity

THAT FINAL DAY ON MT. KILIMANJARO was my threshold crossing. I surrendered to everything opening up inside me as I completed my pilgrimage down the mountain. I wasn't the same woman who had begun the climb. "Donna, love yourself first, and great love will follow!" Halmouth said to me during my descent. That chance meeting felt anything but chance, and his transmission of self-love was my call to action. He'd been able give it to me because I was ready to live from a deeper, softer place inside me, and I was beginning to see how the harder, pushing parts of me no longer fit with who I was becoming.

"I need to share this adventure with many women!" I told Maria when she met us in Arusha at the hotel we stayed at the night after our climb. The following day, Maria took our whole group, exhausted but happy, to see the boarding school where the young African girls learned leadership skills through the Kisa Project. The high school girls were happy to see us and hear about our climb. They too wanted to climb Kili like their mentors, Assinawae and Hadija, who were with us. I felt buoyed up by their joy. Our Colorado team of climbers plus five African girls (Ellie came back and shared the day with us) visited three schools that day and held the hands of these young women all day long as we saw their classrooms, dorms, chemistry labs, and chapel. We had all touched into a greater expression of gratitude, generosity of spirit, and authentic self-expression that day.

I took their sense of empowerment deeply into my heart and body, where it resonated with what I was feeling inside myself. I felt that my call was to guide other women to find empowerment in their lives, to lead women through challenging life events and help them find the inner tools to grow and become more resilient, which was what the African girls were learning. I began in earnest to share my slideshow, the story of my trip, and my vision for how I wanted to offer adventure retreats and trips to groups of women in midlife.

Ani Liggett, a Boulder therapist and the author of *Endings. Beginnings . . . When Midlife Women Leave Home in Search of Authenticity*, wrote that it took a lot of courage to follow the call to authenticity. She spoke of the many pressures women felt to stay in the mold and not venture out to explore more of themselves. I felt those pressures coming up in me when I returned from my Kilimanjaro climb. I was finally finding my truth, my authentic self as a woman, but I was also feeling the pull to stay in my comfy life. I wanted more adventure and a way to serve, but I noticed how hard it was to stand tall in that spot. I had to sit longer in my meditation practice to take in and allow the awakening that was happening inside me. I wondered how a person carried such a spiritual experience back into their day-to-day life.

When I returned home from the trip, I collapsed into the quiet aloneness of my new home. I was living alone for the first time since my twenties. Earlier in my life, loneliness and depression would easily creep back in unconsciously. But I was no longer unconscious, so I began to mindfully work with my pattern of beliefs about feeling lonely and alone. I identified the beliefs that were causing judgment about being alone. Did I think something about me was unlovable? A part of me *felt* unlovable, but I also felt a powerful new part of me coming forth that was real and alive, and I wanted to let her out more. It was interesting to me that my self-critic was no longer shouting at me. I had successfully moved her over by befriending her. She was now my coach, urging me forward to discover all of me inside and nudging me to continue to unburden and heal the part that felt unlovable. She was totally on my team now.

I began in earnest to share my slideshow, the story of my trip, and my vision for how I wanted to offer adventure retreats and trips to groups of women in midlife. My vision began to unfold when I met Susie, a nature guide and coach from Eagle who was interested in collaborating with me. She had been through a difficult divorce earlier in her life, had raised two daughters, and lived on a beautiful ranch where she did retreats for women and young girls. Our visions were closely aligned around helping midlife women grow through major challenges in life using the vehicle of nature adventures where they had to expand, face their fears, feel their feelings, and get unstuck. We put together tools we each could teach these women through experiences in nature.

I looked up at Susie, my coleader and river guide, as she pulled the newly inflated "duckie" (inflatable kayak intended for whitewater use) into the water next to the others that had been placed there by the rafting company hosting our day on the Colorado River. She was going to lead the first day of our four-day adventure retreat in Eagle, Colorado, which we were calling "Courageous Transitions."

"Now step into the water, ladies, and feel the power of the river," Susie said as she walked into the river. As the current flowed up against her legs, she turned back toward our group of three women standing in life jackets on the river's edge. They seemed less timid than I would have expected. I stepped into the water myself and moved toward Susie as she continued to talk.

"The river has so much to teach us about moving through difficult objects and challenges. We can explore this by being with the river and learning to read its path. Feel the power of the current through your body and get familiar with how to be with the river to let it guide you, not frighten you."

The women stepped in too, getting wet up to their waists and allowing the river to work on them. I felt it too, and I saw what Susie was teaching: a deep wisdom of being with the river. I lifted my arms up, as if in celebration of the river, and cheered. The other women followed my lead, and we moved into the water a bit deeper. Then we created a circle and held hands. This moment felt like the beginning of our group spirit building together, and I smiled as I looked back at Susie. She had joined in too and slowly guided us back up to the boats, where we had left our gear, water, and lunch.

"Donna, you take up the rear, and I'll head out with the first two duckies with Sharon and Jaime."

We had already determined who we thought would be the strongest in their individual duckies, so Sharon, Jaime, and Susie launched and I remained on the shore with Janet. Janet had asked to have some extra support, so I was going to stay with her.

Janet gingerly stepped into her duckie as I held it for her. She was in her early sixties and had just lost her husband of thirty years. She was in full-blown grief, but she was ready to face it and move through it. My heart was open for her, and I saw the determination on her face.

"I know I can do this," she said. "I just need to go a bit slowly until I feel more comfort in the boat." She took the paddle and started maneuvering it through the very gentle waves to the eddy and down the river toward the others. Susie had instructed us to follow the currents, stay on the top of the wave trains, and watch for eddies to pull us out where we could rest if need be. I could tell that Janet was studying the river as I paddled up alongside her and settled into an easy stroke with her. We were launched and on our way!

Up ahead, we were coming to our first set of easy rapids, and Susie lead the group so they could watch her as she headed through them. Sharon and Jaime both scrambled a bit to get their boats in the right wave train, but they did and followed each other through. I waved at them with a thumbs up as Janet headed toward the rapids. I saw her arm shaking a bit as she dipped the paddle into the water and tried to pull harder, and I moved my duckie closer to her, encouraging her to keep going. She popped onto the wave train just as her duckie twisted backwards and rolled through the waves that way. I smiled at her confidently as she kept paddling and turned herself around, ending the rapids facing forward again.

"See, you did just fine, Janet," I called out to her. "Great recovery."

She looked pretty proud of herself and paddled on to catch up with the rest of the group.

We managed to hit a big windstorm as we neared our lunch stop. We had just gone through the biggest rapids of the day, and we were all pretty worn out because the wind had been with us all morning. Susie pulled her duckie to the boat ramp and stepped out, signaling that we all needed to head over to the ramp and beach our own boats. We pulled the duckies up out of the water, and while some of us looked for a picnic table, others went over to the support vehicle we had left at the lunch stop to get more jackets.

As we were cleaning up after lunch, Janet came over to me. "I'm pretty wiped out. Do you think we could call it a day?"

"That was a rough wind, wasn't it? But you did so well through those rapids!"

She smiled as a well-earned glow filled her face.

I thought we'd accomplished a lot on the river thus far. "I'll check with the rest of the group and see what everyone else thinks."

I spoke privately with Susie. "What do you think about calling it a day? Janet is pretty wiped out, even though she did an amazing job—as did the others. But this wind! I wonder how the others would feel if we went home early."

"Well, we certainly could do that. Luckily, we have our van here. I don't think the other women would be too upset. It's a long way to the final destination today, and this wind is just getting stronger. I think it's the right plan, Donna, but let's talk it over with the group and let them decide."

"Just another opportunity to learn how to work with bumps in the road when they appear in life, right?"

When we got back to the group, Susie started the conversation. "Ladies, what a great job you have all done on the river so far. How did you like the rapids?" She looked over at Sharon and Jaime, who were shivering and wrapped up in a raincoat they were sharing.

"I loved paddling through them and realized how fun they were when I stopped being scared," Jaime said. And since she had never acted scared, it was fun for us to hear that revelation from her.

"I think the river was speaking to us today," Sharon added. "I personally got so much, and I'm a bit worn out. Those rapids were really fun, though."

"What about you, Janet?" Susie asked, nudging her to share her experience with the other women.

"I learned how to move through my fear even though it was tough in moments out there. Donna helped me by staying nearby. But I personally have had enough. I'm wiped out."

"What do the rest of you think about ending our trip here today?" Susie asked as she looked over at me. She was timing her comments to fit the flow of the conversation.

Sharon and Jaime looked at each other and then back at us. "We're okay with that plan, Susie," Sharon said. "This was all I needed, and I feel inspired and happy."

I stayed with the group to finish up cleaning after lunch while Susie went over to get the van. I was thinking how serendipitous it was that we had left the van there. Susie had suggested it as a possible plan, and it had been the right thing to do. Taking the river all the way to the final takeout was way too much for the group that day. I was very relieved because I needed to have energy and strength to get through the rest of the day to facilitate our discussion on what we'd learned on the river.

Later, after outdoor showers and rest, Susie and I began cooking dinner in the outdoor kitchen. There was a tarp tent covering the area, which included a picnic table, so when it started to rain a bit, we were dry. Even though the wind had died by then, the clouds looked a bit ominous and grey. Our retreat schedule allowed for lots of connection time and personal sharing at meals, along with ceremony and process time after dinner.

After dinner, in the glow of the sunset, Susie and I facilitated the discussion about our day on the river with the retreat participants. Sitting on blankets and BackJack chairs around the grassy circle that was our sacred space sat Janet, Sharon, and Jaime. We incorporated Native American wisdom traditions by smudging each other with sage as we entered the space and opening our sharing circle by honoring the four directions. Then we asked what they wanted to share about how the experience on the river had impacted them.

As I watched each woman share, I felt opened up and warmed by their hearts and by how they were facing and working with their own challenges through the river experience. The day had been a deep dive into herself for each woman.

Sharon spoke of how much more courageous she felt after learning how to read the river and ride the wave train. She had come to the retreat because divorce had left her feeling depressed and stuck, and she felt she was breaking through those feelings.

Jaime was noticing her increased ability to feel her fear in her body and stand up to it like she did standing in the current and facing each rapid with her duckie. She was feeling calmer about going back to her life as a single mom caregiving her elderly mother in her home with her teenage daughter.

When we got to Janet, she was softly crying, trying to hold back her emotional response to the day. She was moved by a lot and wanted to release it all, so we sat quietly with her and witnessed her emotions. She was able to cry more freely in that sacred space and allow kindness to pour into her from all of us. When she looked up and smiled at us, no words seemed necessary.

It was time for me to speak. I stood up and put my hands on my heart. "Each of you has touched me so deeply on this day. Your courage, your strength, and how you faced your fear head-on was powerful to watch. Thank you for sharing so much of yourselves with us today."

As I sat down, Susie moved closer into the circle and we all held hands. It was dusk and time to complete our process. She looked directly at each woman, starting with Janet, who was closest to her, and then around the circle, acknowledging each woman's words and the deep courage they had shared. Then she said, "So be it. *Aho*. With these words we bless these brave spirits and ask for guidance as we walk together tomorrow on our healing path." When she let go of our hands, she walked over to pick up her lighting stick and brought fire to the center of the circle where there was a fire pit. We all watched in silence as she brought the ceremony to a close.

As Susie and I processed the day later in her cabin, we both realized how powerful it had been for the women. We noticed how much more present and alive we all were, and we were all primed to face our second day on retreat. We felt our decision to leave the river early had been successful.

The next day was rock climbing on a rock wall at Camp Hale, a short drive from our retreat location in Eagle, and more alone time in nature in the afternoon back at camp. On our final morning, the women left Eagle with tears and much empowerment to move their lives forward. Susie and I felt the river and our experiences with it had been the best metaphor for moving the retreatants through their major midlife transitions, so we decided to keep the duckies and the river day as a part of any retreat we would hold again. And we decided to take some time to see what was coming up as our next steps together.

There was much to process about my first experience of coaching midlife women in nature. So much of it felt good and right. But the relationship pieces of the work—collaborating with another coach and nature guide—seemed challenging. I needed to be sure that the retreats were going in the right direction for my work, and I wanted to be really clear with Susie about how we collaborated and shared our tools with the women. So we deepened our relationship together by taking a course on creating powerful retreats as we began to plan the next year of nature retreats we wanted to jointly offer.

Chapter Seventeen

The Deep Dive through Grief

GRIEVING OUR LOSSES AT MIDLIFE is the way to find our paths to authenticity and the creation of a new version of ourselves. Learning how to grieve by allowing the space and time in our lives to let it happen is transformational by itself for women. As the great Vietnamese Buddhist teacher Thich Nhat Hahn puts it, no mud, no lotus. Just as the mud allows the lotus to grow and bloom, so too can the painful parts of our lives bring the opportunity for growth. When we are not afraid to feel the pain and go into the "mud" as it shows up in and around our bodies, we can transmute it into new insights and new identities we couldn't see or experience before. By diving deep within ourselves, we can address our inner being's desire for integration and wholeness.

One cool December, I looked out at the frosty but clear morning and began my usual morning routine with Millie, my older but still spirited companion Aussie dog, to start my day out in nature with a mindful walk. I dressed warmly in hiking shoes, a wind topper, and a warm hat and headed out the door with Millie, who was unleashed ahead of me. Catching up with her, I clicked in the leash to her collar, picked up her poop, and headed down the driveway and into the path toward the open space. We both needed to get out first thing in the morning now that winter was settling in.

The days were getting darker and shorter, and that impacted my mood, even though I didn't want to admit it. Walking through the fallen leaves, I felt the crunch of dying and decaying matter all around me. I loved this time of year, really. I was calmed by the slow decline of summer brightness into fall's solitude. It awakened within me the familiar cycle of death leading to rebirth—winter giving forth to bursting spring—and I was hoping I could leave some of the darkness I'd been feeling since holding the women's retreat months earlier and rebirth into something fresh as I planned the next one. I had dropped into the past a bit more during the fall, especially on my mindful walks, where I consciously gave myself more time to grieve. I knew there was more to let out, and giving myself time to allow the feelings to surface was one way I knew how to grieve.

My past grieving had happened when feelings flowed out in situations that surprised me, like when I moved in with Brett and realized I hadn't grieved the end of my marriage to Peter. Or when I finally realized I couldn't appreciate the gifts I'd received from my mom until she was gone. But now I was choosing to create time for the feelings to come up and process through because I wanted to fully heal. And I knew I wasn't through it all.

Millie ran over to the edge of the irrigation ditch that she loved to drink from all summer long. It was all dried up now, and she stopped and looked back at me as if to say, "What happened to my drinking stream?" Then she left it just as easily as the idea to drink from it had arrived. And with amazing equanimity, she stepped out again, leading me on the trail with a knowing and trust that water would appear again soon.

I'd learned so much about managing my reactivity by watching my dog. That morning I was reacting to the appearance of sadness within me again. Even though I had invited it, I could feel that parts of me still resisted it.

More sadness, still?

Yes, more to learn from, I replied to that part, smiling at the familiar cacophony of voices inside me that I had learned to hear.

Yes, Brett and I had trained Millie together, and she was loyal to both of us. She loved us both thoroughly. Since the divorce, we shared her, passing her back and forth between our homes. She was my reminder of the past as well as the symbol of the new life I was carving out. In some ways, she represented all things transitional, but she provided something more: the opportunity to love and be loved.

The previous night had been rough. I had cried myself to sleep again. Missing connection and tenderness, I tried to comfort myself with a hot bath and a good read. I brought in soothing touch and wrote in my journal about my feelings. I missed a family—my family. Julian was far away, living in Chicago. I was missing him, and I had sobbed softly. The second family I had worked so hard to create with Brett, Julian, and Alex was now nonexistent. I was alone again, and I had never wanted to be alone. The feeling of aloneness I'd felt as a single mom crept back in, and I wondered where and how I'd been triggered again.

I remembered that past August. Julian and I had been invited on a family trip to Maine with Martha and Joe's family and friends. They had rented a house on the coast near Portland. I was emotional that week and couldn't stop crying. Being with family again and feeling the loss of my own immediate family was almost too real to face, and my grief unraveled.

I projected a lot onto my sister, feeling like I was a little girl again and she was my mother, unable to tolerate my deep feelings. Martha was very patient and loving, but I couldn't see it or trust it. I had dropped into my little girl part again, and she clearly had more to cry about. She needed to be allowed to cry, be messy, and feel loved in the process—just loved. My family, a more aware and attuned family now, held me lovingly that week, and I was very grateful. They had supported me through a lot, and I was getting what I needed to move on in my life.

Later, when I got home and allowed it to settle, I saw all of it with more clarity, and I understood more deeply how my parts were coming together into a new wholeness. That round of grieving was similar to the ones before. Another rebirthing was happening, and I was feeling it as new energy and creativity moving me forward. This time, it was more subtle and deeper in the way it was guiding me.

A vision began to materialize as a longing to help other women like me learn how to face and process through their own grief. It seemed to be the key to moving forward in *my* life, and I saw many women in my practice get stuck because they were afraid of going into that pain. They were afraid it would be so big that they would either never get out of it or get stuck in sadness and depression. I knew that one could get stuck in a depression loop, but I also knew that learning to break out of the depression loop and feel sadness was key to moving through grief.

I wanted to show more women how to feel their feelings of sadness, despair, and hopelessness through their bodies, not their minds. Mindfulness and yoga had taught me how to embody my feelings and let my body process through them completely. Our bodies knew how to do that and we just had to learn to trust them.

Helping women complete their healing path and go forward out of their grief meant teaching them about the silver lining: a more resilient and more authentic woman would emerge. It also meant teaching them how to use the tools to embody their pain and transmute it. I was hoping I could create a retreat that would unfold pieces or parts of the process for women in challenging midlife transitions.

I had put together a five-step "midlife voyage to transformation" program from my own healing work with IFS, from using mindful self-compassion tools with others, and from working with many clients as they healed from their grief. I had created a new website where I could share that five-step model with other women. Now I wanted to teach this model more directly.

The following spring I met with Susie to rework our Courageous Transitions retreat for women, adding more of my tools and again creating adventures in nature as opportunities for grief work. Both of us realized that finding a way to grieve our losses was the key to moving our own lives forward, and we were in alignment about wanting to help other women learn how to do that for themselves.

It was day three of our four-day women's retreat, and I was leading the four women up the final physical event: climbing Heart Mountain, a steep two-mile hike up through the red clay and transitional flora of the pinyon-juniper woodlands, so distinct in that part of Colorado and so different from the familiar conifer forests of ponderosa pines and Douglas fir I was used to at higher elevations. As I walked up the gravel road along the ranch, I noticed Kristy and Judy walking together, and I slowed down.

"I don't know if I can do this, Donna," Kristy gasped as she came up to me. "This is a lot for me today."

I guessed the breathing was her way of trying to communicate her fear and ambivalence about doing the hike. She had said it was a big physical challenge for her.

"Hey, you're *here*, Kristy! It's one step at a time."

"But I'm holding so much pain today. It's all coming up."

"Well, keep holding it as you walk, dear. And bring in that kindness you need to help you." I wasn't going to let her rely on me for answers and help too much because I had observed that pattern in her the previous day when we'd taught mindful self-compassion skills. I wanted her to use her own skills to hold herself. "You've let out so much already that I suspect you're more than halfway through."

I was referring to the grief and pain she had come to the retreat to learn how to release. In our circle the previous day, she had shared the real facts about her deep grief: Her wife was dying of Alzheimer's and she was trying to accept it, but she was fighting it all the way. A year earlier, Kristy's wife had retired from an intense job, planning to enjoy her golden years with Kristy. And then she was diagnosed with Alzheimer's disease. Kristy's grief counselor, with whom she had been working for over a year, suggested she come on the retreat to help her learn acceptance, the final stage of grieving when we actually allow the feelings to process through into a new place. I felt she need-ed to be able to release her guilt before she could let go so self-compassion could help her find self-forgiveness.

Meanwhile, Judy was beside Kristy, quietly focusing on her moving feet and her breathing, totally going inward, as she had been doing on the retreat. It was a survival strategy. Her chal-lenge was to learn how to not be so internal and carried away by the confusion of it all. Her husband's sudden death four months earlier was such a provoking mystery to her, and learn-ing to speak about what was happening—to name it and befriend it—was not happening yet. She was doing what was called "spiritual bypassing" and using her spiritual practices as a way of avoiding feeling her deep sorrow.

Judy was just starting her grief process in the first two stages of the midlife voyage I called "Lost at Sea" and "Finding a Mooring." Every time she seemed to find some grounding, some way to connect with her grieving self, she retreated back into her distractions—essentially being lost at sea again. I had seen her do it twice in the past two days.

I leaned forward and pointed to my left. Then I turned and started walking on the trail to Heart Mountain. The other women followed. The trail passed through a forest of Gambel oak that created a canopy over the juniper and sage shrubs we were walking through. I used the rest step slowly and carefully to find the right pace for the grieving women. They fell in line, putting one foot slowly in front of the other through the steep first half mile and stepping around the cryptobiotic soil growing along the path. I had learned about the phenomenon of bacteria, lichen, and moss growing in the soil on my first trip to Arches National Park and Moab years earlier. It was important to avoid stepping on the soil in which they grew because you could kill the organisms growing there. As I walked around it, the other women followed my lead.

Susie and the other two women caught up, and we all settled into quietness, as if the forest had called us to do so. It was a way of offering solace and peace with which we could quicken our spirits into deeper healing and love. That was how I felt when I went into nature. It was an opportunity to drop deeper into the love that the trees and sky held out for me without asking for anything in return. Climbing mountains was just an extension of that experience for me, and I was sharing it with other women now.

Susie was talking with Val and Jen, the younger two women on the retreat who were just beginning midlife. Both were getting divorced. "Let yourselves drop into this experience now, and let nature do its work on you."

Susie and I both taught the deep healing power of nature and experiences in nature to transform us. She had introduced me to this special hike up Heart Mountain when we first planned to do a retreat together.

Leading the group, I turned a corner and glanced up at a massively expanding mature Gambel oak that had lost all of its leaves but was still standing strong, offering comfort and strength in the shadows. I stood under her for a moment and felt her glorious power and then invited Kristy to step into her embrace as I moved out of it. In the silence, we both felt the tree's gift to us. When Susie walked by the tree behind Val and Jen, she hugged the trunk and picked up a rock that was nestled in its y-shaped trunk.

"Another heart-shaped rock has just been offered to us by this beautiful oak tree. Keep looking for the magic coming to you here," she said as she handed the heart-shaped rock to Jen, who had stopped to look. I kept moving, carrying the group upward until we finally got to a clearing where we could look down on the valley below. I stopped and let the group catch their breath.

Judy came to stand next to me, and we looked out over the Eagle Valley. We could see the massive Gore Range and higher mountains in the distance with the Eagle River running through the valley below.

She turned to me and said, "I didn't realize how much I needed to get away from everything until now. I was on automatic pilot. I think I'm feeling something different today, and it's exciting."

I put my hand on her shoulder. "I'm so glad you're here, Judy. Just keep noticing it all."

We turned to go, and Susie spent a few minutes checking in with Val and Jen before we headed up the final stretch, which was steep and rocky. Kristy was getting her bearings and walking more deliberately, like she was enjoying the hike more. Susie, Val, and Jen walked past her and took the lead, leaving Judy and me to take up the rear.

I watched Kristy stay in her body and keep her pace up, not being distracted by the younger women moving through the hike at a faster pace. I loved seeing that lack of competition, and I loved seeing her connection with her inner self grow on the retreat. She had reacted to things Jen and Val had said and done the first two days of the retreat, but now she was changing that. She was dropping down deeper into herself where she needed to meet her grief. She was doing her work.

As we neared the corner to step up and over a log and onto the final ledge to the top, Jen and Val pounded triumphantly up to the top and disappeared up there. Slowly and deliberately, Judy followed Kristy as they made the final moves to get to the top themselves. When they stepped on the ledge, I was right behind them as they grabbed hands and hugged each other. Great celebration followed as Susie joined us, finding room around the big rock outcropping that was shaped like a heart.

Susie shared a prayer and a blessing. "May we all be held in the embrace of this heart mountain and feel her power. Each of you can stand here, looking out, and place a rock on her face and make your own wish. Bring in this mountain's love to yourself. By climbing this mountain, you have opened up more space inside yourself for all that you need to hold. Now you can begin to hold it all."

The women slowly took turns making their wishes out over the rock and into the valley below them, and I could feel their pride and determination pouring forth. It was very empowering to get to the top of Heart Mountain with a group like this.

Kristy, ready to expand more, walked up the small knoll behind the rock ledge we were all on and explored more of the top of the peak. As I remembered, it was wooded and flat up there for a while before you got to the other side. Soon, all of us began wandering. I came to a stand of Gambel oak trees that were tall and massive, and I was moved to climb one of them. When I got to the top, I could see so much more, and it was exhilarating.

I yelled to the group to come over and climb the other trees nearby. Susie and I took turns helping the women climb up into the trees. The one I climbed was too hard for Kristy, but she found the right one for her, moved up into its forked trunk quickly, and then headed up another foot into the branches. She didn't need any help at all. She was so excited that she could climb up quickly on her own that she was giddy with joy. It was fun to see her like that, and we all reveled in her joy. When she came down, we all headed back down the mountain in silence, as if we had a lot to process inside ourselves. I certainly felt that way.

It was designated free time when we returned from the hike. The retreatants used that "alone time," as we called it, for journaling, meditation, sitting in nature, or other solo activities. Susie and I took advantage of the quiet to connect, process, and plan our final evening ceremony and closing for the retreat. We had planned a "threshold crossing ceremony" to start at 6:00 p.m., right after dinner. We hoped the women would share what they'd learned during the retreat as a part of that ceremony.

Susie, dressed in a warm Indian poncho with a skirt and tights underneath, stepped into the sacred circle she had just opened by smudging all of us with sage and lighting the candle in the center of the circle. We all turned to face each of the four cardinal directions, following her lead as she honored them. Then we reached down to the ground to honor the great Mother Earth and looked up, raising our palms to Father Sky.

My heart warmed each time we did this traditional Native American opening to our ceremonies.

I looked over at Kristy on my right and Judy across from me, wondering what was bubbling up inside them. I loved how it always seemed to unfold mysteriously at every retreat. We moved into the ceremony as Susie talked about our three big days and the struggles and learnings that had come to pass. My job was to hold the space and offer support. I was doing that.

"Now it's time for each of you to share what is appearing, as best you can, and let it become your truth. Who would like to start here at the threshold? I'll guide you to your crossing."

Judy stepped up first. "I'm ready!" She walked over to the log Susie had put down to represent the threshold. "I feel like a new woman tonight. Today's hike was my breakthrough moment. I realized I no longer need to hide in automatic pilot mode. I think I was shutting myself off from taking anything else in. You all helped me open the door to my grief, and I saw it all today." She stopped and gasped, putting her hands over her face. Then she dropped down to a kneeling position and sobbed. We were silent witnesses to her breakthrough. In a few minutes, she stopped and wiped her face, stood up, and walked across the threshold proudly. We clapped, and she walked back to her spot in the sacred circle we had drawn together.

We sat in silence again. Then Val walked to the center and placed her hand over her heart. "I didn't know I could bring in kindness to myself like I did today. Finding a way to hold myself in a loving embrace with self-compassion and stop beating myself up inside as I walked at what was the right pace for me was an amazing breakthrough. I've always pushed myself to exhaustion, and even though I pushed it at the top of Heart Mountain today, I didn't push in my normal way. I was kinder to myself. Thanks y'all!" She again held her hand on her heart as she walked over the threshold, paused with her back to us, crossed, and lifted her hands in the air. We all clapped for her.

Jen completed her threshold crossing process next, silently but powerfully. It was very moving to watch her work through the many emotions she was feeling as she crawled and rolled over and over on the grass and then released the emotions at the end in sobs that turned into a more peaceful, calming position of Savasana. I could tell she did a lot of yoga and knew how to process with it.

And then we all sat quietly waiting for Kristy. Darkness was almost upon us, and she was crying softly in the dark shadows growing in the background. Then she stood up and slowly walked to the center of the circle, glancing over at me as she walked past. I focused on her eyes and sent loving kindness wishes to her as she began to speak.

"You all have given me so much—each of you. I was broken, and you helped me heal. I cried, and you held me with your hearts. I feel that somehow I have found a path forward through this stuff I'm so stuck in. I'm breaking through it somehow." She lifted an arm and marched over the threshold, lifting her fists and pushing away what she called her "stuckness." When she got over the log, she turned and looked back at us, and her expression said it all. She was smiling and radiant.

Chapter Eighteen

Rebirthing the New You

UNDERNEATH ALL THE PAIN and messiness of our emotional reactions to traumatic events is the body's response to it all: a cleansing and a rebirthing that allows us to feel new energy and a new response to life. Down in the messy emotions are new parts of us we can begin to feel as we clear out the old patterns and release beliefs that are no longer serving us. Finding what is stuck and breaking through it is how we rebirth ourselves.

New research is showing how this works and how emotions are energy in our bodies that get trapped in our cells. When we grieve, we must go deeply enough into our blockages and resistance to release and transform those emotions. This is something I have learned from my own experience with grief and from working with clients using IFS to heal their burdened exiles, or younger parts.

But I was also learning about rebirthing, as I was calling it, through the awakening that was happening inside me. Slowly, I had learned to listen and pay attention to how this guidance was coming in rather than trying to figure it out or even plan for it. This was not a cognitive process. I was being kinder to myself, both internally and externally, since my Mindful Self-Compassion teacher training in 2015, becoming a teacher of that program, and feeling the self-trust that happened after climbing Kili.

That all coalesced in the creation of a new woman's group: Rebirthing the New Authentic You. So much clarity came to me about the process of rebirthing when I taught this course for the first time in the spring of 2016 to four women. I cataloged the tools for rebirthing as (1) listening for the call of authenticity, (2) awakening your little ones (exiled parts) by allowing your longings and passions to reappear, (3) radically accepting who you are becoming, and (4) retelling your story with your new truth coming forward. I started the group by teaching the women how to create sacred space so that each woman could create an actual space—a compassion container for herself in her home—from which to practice the self-compassion tools on a daily basis.

On the third weekly session, after the four women shared their struggles with creating their own sacred spaces and doing a daily practice, we moved into grief work. To get the women more in touch with their grief, I focused on the second tool (awakening your little ones) with a passion wheel art experience during which they found or drew pictures that evoked an internal unmet longing.

As we processed the experiences of doing their passion wheels, Katy, a ski instructor who was facing two knee replacements, promptly shared that she was clear she was just there to grieve her loss of the ability to use her knees and body teaching skiing. Cathy, a professional writer struggling with burnout and confusion about her future, saw a younger part of herself in the process of trying to write stories when her family was blind to her desire. Maura, who was caretaking a husband whose mental illness left him unable to work, was frustrated by her inability to see or feel anything she longed for in her past. She badly wanted to break through that block. Katy was quietly witnessing and listening to the others while visibly holding herself in self-compassion with hands on her heart, as she had learned to do in the group.

Katy came back the next week bubbling with a new discovery. "My mom was unable to see who I was back then. I was taking care of her anxiety for so long that I never really got to be athletic or active. I was emotionally taking care of her. But now, with my wonderful husband, I get to be me and ski and teach this joyful thing I love. Now I'm afraid I'll lose myself again and be unable to ski." Maura and Cathy asked her to explain more about her discovery, and she talked about the "little girl" part she was seeing and feeling inside her that grew up in her family of origin.

Katy had a lot to share at the next group session. She was already learning about her exiled parts, so she was a bit ahead of the rest of the group. This session was about learning the internal family system (IFS) of parts, simplified into experiencing "head parts" (protective parts) and "body parts" (exiled parts), which would help the group members identify their grieving parts more clearly. We danced and moved together, finding and feeling with our bodies how the parts were showing up inside us. Each of the women was able to draw some of the "head parts" running their life and preventing them from seeing the "little girl" parts underneath that were often found in the body parts.

As they used pastels and charcoal to draw depictions of the parts coming forth, their awareness of them began to grow. They developed curiosity and self-compassion through this IFS exercise, paving the way for the unfolding of their authentic expressions to come forth.

It was in the final session of the eight-week group that more clarity emerged for the group members. The closeness that had developed in our journey together and in the deep sharing that was a part of it had ignited their grieving processes. They had moved deeper within themselves to their painful "little ones," and in the process had discovered blocking parts that needed to be befriended. As we guided each other to learn to recognize their resistance/blocking parts, they could shift their systems and new truths could be revealed

In the final week, I asked the women to rewrite their stories. When they had completed them, I asked who wanted start by reading her new story. Maura stepped up to do that. "I see how and why I have had to block out so much in my life. It was too painful to feel it all. And my husband's illness seemed too hard for me to feel, so I was again blocking everything. I now see that I can feel my own pain and I can see how I am suffering by holding it all back. I'm ready to feel the feelings stuck inside me, and I'm ready to release myself to be alive again."

Cathy's story was a new truth she had learned about herself: that she needed to go slower to actually feel more of what was coming up for her. She had been trying to figure it all out in her head. She shared that she was now connected to her younger self and holding her with lots of love.

And Katy was seeing her wholeness in a deeper way, as well as the part of her that had taken care of her mom. She had befriended that part and recruited her to take care of herself through her upcoming surgery.

As we completed our group together, each woman seemed to be on her rebirthing path to finding a new and more authentic expression of herself in her present life transition.

Meanwhile, I was on a similar path in my life, listening closely to my internal system for the parts that were emerging from my transition of leaving my marriage. While going to the United Church of Christ church, which I had attended with Brett during our marriage, the assistant pastor, with whom I had deeply shared, suggested that I consider getting a spiritual director. As I was leaving that church community, she pulled me aside and said, "Now is the perfect time to explore this deeper you, Donna."

I had heard about spiritual direction from Maria while we were talking about next steps for each of us after the Kilimanjaro trip. I told her about my IFS journey and how it had helped me, and she shared how spiritual direction had guided her through her transitions. Something opened up inside me in that expanded place after that climb, and I could feel a younger part moving forward, calling to me. I realized that I had uncovered another "little girl"—my spiritual seeker. I was very curious and ready to befriend her.

Now that I was going through more grieving with my divorce, I was glad I had my spiritual director Joanne to help me hold this part and listen to her. I shared my Internal Family Systems process with her and *The Spirit-Led Life*, a book written by a Christian minister turned IFS therapist I had met at a Chicago training. Joanne found IFS so helpful that she integrated it into her ministry work. All my parts felt even more understood because of Joanne's receptivity to and curiosity about IFS.

Our work together allowed me to befriend this deeper spiritual seeker part and give her a strong voice now that it was safe for her to be recognized in me, both internally and externally. Talking to Joanne allowed me to integrate my parts into the new woman I was becoming.

I shared with her about how spiritual practices such as meditation and yoga had helped me find my authentic self much more than the worship or group gatherings that happened at the UCC church.

After many attempts at talking to my new pastor, visiting other churches, and exploring opportunities, I was still feeling a disconnect. I was involved in activism for climate change, and I jumped in deeper with more passion to help. My desire to serve was a direct result of my deeper inner work. I was feeling called to teach mindfulness practices more directly in my work and to find Buddhist teachers who could help me deepen my practices, understand my yearning, and find a path to greater service.

I did just that and joined a Buddhist sangha that was designed to guide us in our practices and to apply the Buddhist principles in our lives. Joanne was totally supportive of this new direction for me because she was being led to listen to what was coming next for me. That she was inclusive and accepting of my path into Buddhism was powerful for me.

My new spiritual growth took me away from working with Susie and into a new opportunity I never would have expected. One day in early June, I was invited to attend a work day at the new Rocky Mountain Ecodharma Retreat Center located on 180 acres of private river, meadow, and woodland just a short distance from the Indian Peaks Wilderness. Local dharma teachers had found the property and raised enough money to buy it and the historic buildings on the property. Now we were all joining in to do extra work on the grounds and main lodge because the place was getting remodeled and ready to be used as a retreat center for the first time that summer.

Johann, who had found the land and initiated the purchase and development of the center, was leading our trail building group that day. We were building a beautiful new trail in the most distant part of the property. Five of us worked on the trail crew, and even though Johann had led us all there, I was feeling held and connected by the others in our group too. We connected deeply to our love of the organization's mission: a nature-based retreat center we could all attend and enjoy that was close to home.

Johann turned to me as we were completing our lunch. "Donna, we have an opening in October on the schedule. You could do a woman's retreat up here."

I was surprised by how his words landed inside me. My spiritual part was cheering a yes.

With that invitation, I moved the idea around in my body and heart and decided to take that big step of leading my own retreat for women there. I started planning my Woman's Mindfulness Retreat for that October.

The four-day retreat did not begin until midday because an early snowstorm had left the roads snow-packed at that altitude. With the help of my retreat manager, Jody, we got all fourteen participants settled into their rooms. As they checked in, we assigned yogi jobs and bell ringer jobs to each retreatant as is the tradition for meditation retreats that had been adopted at the Center. I hoped this helped the women feel that each had a way to contribute as they were on retreat by giving some personal time to the whole experience in mindfulness. Even if we were a little late, we were ready to begin.

As I began the first day, I thought about comments several of the women had made in answer to questions asked in the pre-retreat packet I had sent out. They told me they had major challenges in their lives and had come to seek tools for support and guidance. Several had heard of mindfulness but had not explored it, and others had practiced mindfulness before and were looking for more specific tools for self-compassion, like *metta* and other practices specifically designed to help a person cultivate kindness towards themselves when they were feeling challenged. Almost all the women were in major midlife transitions caused by any number of circumstances: retirement;

career changes; husband out of work and struggling; teenagers fighting depression; parents dying; a second baby coming; marital conflict; and/or potential divorce.

As I was creating this mindfulness retreat, I wanted to create the opportunity for women to discover the power of practicing in silence that I had discovered at the first women's retreats I had attended. But the concept of a silent retreat was scary to many of my clients. I decided to create a retreat that offered connection time and time for deeper work in "Noble Silence"—what Buddhists called periods of silent practice during which you kept your gaze down to disconnect from each other. Noble Silence created an opportunity for participants to focus on themselves—to care for themselves. Recent research had shown that women tended to befriend each other and connect socially when they were feeling stressed. I wanted to create the opportunity for women at my retreat to contrast being socially connected and supportive with being quietly focused inward. I had found quiet inward focus to be a path to deeper self-growth for myself.

I started with simple guided mindfulness practices taught with a breath focus and a scientific presentation of mindfulness practices to help the women see their value and to get the women's minds engaged and focused. Later, when the practices began to work their magic, I needed to give less information and could just create the container for the experience to grow deeply into their bodies.

I had planned to teach specific practices designed to cultivate self-compassion in the next two days of the retreat, hopefully ending on Sunday with a variety of practices and experiences that would help the women move through their challenges. I believed that most of them were in what I called stage two of a model I had created describing the stages women in midlife transition went through. That stage was called "finding a mooring," and it preceded stage three, "deep diving." I planned to interview each woman individually, during which I would gather more information, show them my model with its five stages and the tools that aligned with each stage, and confirm that they were at stage two.

On the second day, we put our coats on and went outside on the deck to experience a guided, seated, sensory nature practice. Since this retreat was more mindfulness and less adventure focused, I wanted them to experience the healing power of nature through a pure sensory practice. I guided the women to explore the world outside themselves with their visual, auditory, and gustatory senses and then tap in to their sense of touch and internal feelings. With eyes open, closed, or half-open, we experienced things sensorially, outside the mind's interpretation, as best as we could. I coached them to notice when thinking reappeared and gently bring back the sensory awareness.

Then I invited them to move out into the grounds beyond the lodge. "Let your senses open totally to what is calling out to you— a tree, a pinecone, a flower, or a dead branch—and surrender into the total experience of savoring that gift of nature. Savoring is the mindfulness of positive experience, so allow yourself to totally take the warm positive feelings into your heart and body, just noticing and being with it all. I rang the bell on the edge of the steps of the lodge after thirty minutes had passed to signal the end of the exercise. Hands laden with treasures from nature came into my view, and I lifted my hands in a praying gesture and bowed as they brought their finds into the lodge and placed them on an altar in the Zendo that we had set up just for that. Then we came in and admired it all before our next session.

As I had planned, our third day of practice together was in Noble Silence, which we began at bedtime the night before. At

7:30 the next morning, the wake-up bell ringer walked the halls ringing the bell. By 8:00 we were all settled in the Zendo practicing in silence. I had arrived fifteen minutes early and sat alone in silence in my chair at the front of the room. By the time everyone arrived, I was feeling settled, grounded, and ready to begin.

"This morning, we will start with our compassionate breathing practice," I said. "Please find a comfortable position on either a chair or a cushion. Allow your hips to tip forward a bit so you can find a straighter back. Reaching your head to the sky, lift and find ease in your shoulders as you relax them. Now, take two gentle breaths with me. Breathing in, I feel nurtured. Breathing out, I feel ease. Breathing in, I feel present. Breathing out, I feel calm."

As I continued to lead the practice, I realized that a few women seemed to be missing. Almost before I had another thought, the Zendo door opened and in walked Jody and two others. I wondered if Jody was helping someone needing support. That was our plan, so I decided to look for a written note from her at the next walking meditation break. That was how we communicated during our silent practices.

After eating breakfast in silence, I noticed a few women whispering and looking at each other, not sure how to use the free time they had until our next practice period. Another woman—one who had practiced in silence before—went over to them and held their hands as she gently looked down. She guided them into a silent walking meditation, showing them how to move to their yogi jobs or chores or go outside for a break using that form of mediation. It was the way to take the practice into their lives.

I made a note to explain it more when we had our next walking meditation period. I checked the bulletin board for a message from Jody, found one, and took the time to read her concerns. I was glad I had scheduled private sessions later to support some of the participants.

We had scheduled free time after lunch that we hoped they would spend outdoors in nature. I led some of the women on a short hike in silence near the retreat center buildings. Others more familiar with silent practice wandered farther into the muddy trails slowly melting from the snow earlier in the week. Feeling refreshed, I came back and set up the Zendo with more cushions for our afternoon practices, which started with a Compassionate Body Scan. The power of the silence seemed to be building as I began the practice focused on sensing deeply into bodily sensations while creating an attitude of kindness and curiosity.

"Now bring your focus and breath to the whole right half of your body—the foot, ankle, knee, thigh, and hip—noticing any sensations that may be arising and bringing in kindness to your-self as you notice whatever is there."

My words drifted into the background as a woman close to me began to sob, first quite fitfully and then more quietly, her body rising with each sob and then calming as she came to the end of her release. I think I was touched as much as the rest of the women as she allowed the grief to arise naturally and be released through her body. Later, in our private session, she was able to name the clarity she got through the experience. She was healing a deep wound from her past.

At the end of the day, we formed a circle to do a practice for coming out of silence. I asked the women to connect with each other again with words by whispering to a partner about their experiences in silent practice. When we completed our retreat with a closing circle after dinner, one of the participants stood up to offer her experiences. "I've seen the power of gratitude practices in my life, but learning how to bring in love to myself through self-compassion has given me a more powerful tool. This is a path to our soul."

That comment led to other women sharing their experiences, including how they learned to be curious and explore silence as a way to see deeper into themselves. But mostly, the comments were focused on learning how to be kinder to themselves and how difficult that was for them to do. During the final hours of the retreat, the women spoke powerfully about their experiences.

In this retreat, I was teaching the fuller toolbox of self-compassion practices to give the women the patience and support to go into stage three, deep diving—the process of facing grief head-on. When they were ready to do this grief work, the healing container needed to be well fortified so they would have the patience and support to look deeper under the layers of grief and stay connected to the process instead of running away from it. These practices were creating that stronger mooring—an anchor for going deeper. During the last day of the retreat, I saw that several retreatants were beginning to deep dive into their grief, even though they were unable to talk about it yet.

When I named this stage—finding a mooring—I hadn't realized the inner knowing coming forth as a result of my deeper spiritual practices. Now I did. I realized that when a deeper foundation within oneself was attained, the rest of the stages could flow from that. Grief could not happen unless we had the ability to deeply hold ourselves. And rebirthing could not flow from grieving unless we had the compassion and perspective that came from the deep caring for ourselves that was created in that mooring—our own unique and loving relationship with ourselves. I had stumbled on the tools that would help women get through the scary and difficult deep diving stage—or at least get their toes dangling in the dark waters.

Afterword

I SET OFF WALKING into the forest trail I had longed to walk all year. I needed to nurture myself with the same sensory nature practice I had facilitated with groups. The Ecodharma Retreat Center had been closed because of the pandemic that was sweeping through the world. It had shut down abruptly in March, and I hadn't gotten to attend my spring retreat with my sangha, nor had I been able schedule the retreat I'd planned to conduct in November. Everything had been cancelled. I had requested a solo retreat time at the center because it was a special place I loved.

It was still cold that May morning, and I looked up at the sky, hoping the clouds would break soon so I could see the sun. I headed down the hill, pausing and breathing deeply as I walked across the narrow bridge over the fast flowing St. Vrain river that cut through the property. The river would be here when I came back. But first I needed to visit the forest.

I walked across the damp and soggy meadow to the forest trail, stopping at the forest entrance that always took my breath away. I looked down, pausing to find the familiar signs of the many footprints creating the path, but those signs were hidden by spring snow and the lack of visitors. As I slowly stepped forward, my hiking boot went down into the snow, but I could see the familiar path even with snow on it. I relaxed deeply into the rhythm of the movement, dropping deeper into myself as I walked through the trees and slowly uphill. I knew the path was marked by tiny orange or yellow ribbons, but I couldn't see them, so I let my feet guide me. I felt my parts inside me: courage and excitement, *yirah* bubbling up. Any fear from the past about being in the forest alone was gone. That day, I was loving being alone in that magical forest. I felt my "little girl" parts there too, feeling peaceful and joyous, ready to play in nature.

As I reached what I thought was the place where the path turned west, my eyes were pulled east to a hilly knoll breaking through to the partially clearing sky. In the brighter light I saw some rocks with big trees on them. There was less snow there, so I immediately headed off trail through the forest toward the knoll. I navigated through its rocky base and around the trees. I had to hold onto the biggest tree as I caught my breath, pulling myself up to the ledge where they were growing tall to look out at the view they had. The sentinel trees seemed to be a family of bristlecone pines gathered to watch over the forest. I felt they had called me over, and I got closer.

"How do we go from here?" I asked them. First I looked up at the father tree standing next to me. "What is our appropriate response to the Earth's cry right now? We're facing death because we are creating it as we live in disharmony with each other and with Mother Nature. This pandemic is teaching us so much."

I felt a sense of calm coming from the tree, and I decided to resonate with him. Equanimity and calmness came forth, and I got more curious.

Then I looked at the great mother tree on my left, standing with arms outstretched, and the younger trees down below her looking back at her with their branches and trunks swaying. The sun broke out of the clouds at that moment, and a ray of sunlight poured over the maternal tree. She was clearly protect-ing the younger trees behind me on the ledge with their bright green shoots in their immature cones. I spoke to the young trees as well, thanking them for their energy and enthusiasm, and I reveled in their brightness.

What was coming up was my "little girl" part's voice, loud and clear. "You trees see my truth so clearly. I'm no longer bro-ken and unlovable. I love being witnessed by your loving pres-ence, dear trees. You see my path through grief and unburden-ing to now—to this place of joy and adventure, this place of calm and wholeness."

I reflected on the moment in the past when I was depressed after having Julian, when I was feeling that part's pain so deeply for the first time. I came face-to-face with her in my darkest moments then. She scared me, and I closed off from her, mov-ing on in my life because I did not have the greater ability of my compassionate Self then to hold her and be curious toward her. I brought my hand to my heart and soothed my part with my touch. *You are safe now with me*, I whispered to her. *I see you and I love you.*

As I looked up at the father tree above me, I touched his trunk lovingly. I was feeling the joy I usually felt when I went out in nature—the joy that had been roused on that powerful day at Mt. Madonna when the MBSR practices awakened that part again. The tree showed me the powerful opening to my deepest Self I experienced when I was curious about that joy. *May I be filled with joy*, I said, repeating the *metta* phrase I had written for myself as I continued feeling the loving presence of the tree resonating within me. I was grateful to be able to dive deeper into myself and feel it all. *May I be happy.*

Turning to the mother tree to my left, I looked deeply at her outstretched branches, strong and powerfully holding many additional shoots and branches filled with many leaves and pinecones. The branches were weathered deeply by the wind and weather, and yet they were still reaching out, extending toward the forest and beyond, exuding power, strength, and compassion.

I reflected on my mothering part and how much anger and fear she had to release as a single mom to deepen my capacity to be compassionate, caring, and generous again after my first divorce. I saw my current self in the tree, continuing to use the compassion and curiosity within me to create more self-trust within my body and inner parts so I could keep settling myself down to the tasks of my life and my work. I had to learn how to lovingly hold myself and my parts in compassion, rather than criticism and judgment, to grieve and rebirth myself.

That tree also reflected the healing energy of Mary, Mother of Jesus, that I met in Halmouth coming down from Kilimanjaro, slowly integrating and growing within myself. That healing energy was compassion, the infusion that had brought it all together inside me and which had always been there, just covered up by life's lessons of pain and suffering.

I stepped down from the ledge feeling I was letting the tree's compassionate energy lead me into the next steps of being with all of my parts fully, deeply accepting, allowing, and feeling each of them as I walked. As I got back on the trail and continued to the top of the rise, I became aware of the way that being on Kili with those African girls and male guides—all of them transforming their lives simultaneously—had opened up so much energy inside me so I could better serve others in my life. My deeper, sustained practice of mindfulness was creating the same opening inside me, and in that moment, I knew I was on my new path in my new life. I would continue to follow that desire to serve further, letting the rebirthed and unburdened exiled parts lead my system in a powerful way toward living in generosity and kindness for myself and others and taking action in the world. In essence, once unburdened, the freed "little girl" part had rebirthed into a "spiritual seeker" part.

At the top, I climbed through the trees and up to the rocky ledge overlooking the whole property and beyond it. I looked out west at Mount Audubon in the Indian Peaks covered with snow and ice but shining brightly in the sunshine. I took in a breath and let it settle deeply in a long exhale. There was such beauty in this place to behold. Continuing to feel deep gratitude and joy, my heart broke open even more than it ever had before. I let my feet guide me back down the steep and winding forested trail to the clearing in the meadow, following my memory of the trail rather than the yellow ribbons.

I spent the rest of the day wandering in the meadow, looking for our resident moose and her baby and doing walking meditation along the St. Vrain river bank, which was covered with aspen groves. I finally sat, enjoying the full experience of being with the beautiful natural wonder of the place. I spoke to the river, watching her cascade gently and patiently through what seemed like some big rocks and a narrow chute of downed trees creating a complex but survivable obstacle. If I were navigating this portion of the river from a duckie or boat, I would be fearful. I decided to ask her about this familiar fear coming up again.

"How do I work with my fear?" The river danced and sparkled back at me as she spoke. "Flow with your fear and let it guide you forward and through. Don't let it shut you down. Keep dancing and singing and loving it. Each obstacle washes you through to clarity."

Never before had I felt the love and gratitude I had for these natural wonders coming back at me as in that moment. I stayed there a long time, taking in and savoring what I had felt and experienced that day. I watched the sun begin to set, and then I headed back to the lodge for my last evening there alone, calmed and at peace, feeling a deeper connection to the natural world and universe beyond me than I had ever felt before.

Acknowledgments

WRITING THIS MEMOIR is the result of many years of writing stories from this or that event in my life as a way to process them and integrate them so I could move on in my life. In the process, I realized they were not just helping me. My stories were helping others with their own struggles.

First, I want to thank the members of the First Congregational Memoir Writing Group, which I have facilitated over the past three years, for how they opened their hearts to this process with me. Bimonthly, I sat with these special ones as a group member, and we shared our most vulnerable struggles with each other. I want to thank Anne Weiher, Sheila Evans, Cynthia Tamesue, George Jones, and Emily Wingeier who helped me through my final year of writing. If I hadn't had this powerful witnessing and loving container, I wouldn't have had the courage to take my stories to the next level where I felt they could be most valuable.

How do we find the right stories, and what is the story we really want to tell for a memoir? The discovery of a midlife story that could help other women happened slowly over time. I am very grateful to my friend and colleague, Arielle Schwartz, who supported me by staying with me, steadfastly, through the process and encouraged me to let it develop over time.

Her support led me to Tanja Pajevik, who became my writing coach and developmental editor. Tanja's careful feedback was instrumental in helping me find which stories to include and the arc of time for my midlife focus. Her course and our writer's workshop that came later gave me the support and guidance to complete my second draft and work through the challenges with structure and voice. I want to thank Jessica Stokes for her support in reading chapters, sending feedback, and joining me on this powerful writing journey. But most of all, I want to thank my editor, Melanie Mulhall, for her skill, dedication, and heartful support of this project.

I want to thank my IFS community of trainers, colleagues, and clients who have greatly impacted my story and my personal healing. I'm grateful to Richard Schwartz for his creation of this powerful healing system and for coming to Boulder and introducing me to IFS that first time in 2002.

I want to thank Barb Cargill and Toni Herbine-Blank for their early support in my first Level I training and for their ongoing support as they guided me through additional therapy and trainings to deepen my skill as a trauma therapist and my personal growth as a woman.

I also would like to thank Susan McConnell and Beth O'Neill for early supervision and training in Chicago and Julie Jlona and Mary Steege for deep friendship in Chicago. I also want to thank Mariel Pastor in Portland, Oregon, for encouraging me to branch out to other parts of the country as a program assistant and for inviting me to teach with her in the IFS Level I retreat style format. And I want to thank my Denver/Boulder IFS Family of colleagues who have PA-ed together and have supported our IFS practices and lives through all the midlife struggles we have all shared: Robin Richardson, Stew Brown, Heather Leavesley, Bob Calhoun, and Rebecca Drogan. Also thanks to Elizabeth Taeubert, Rebecca's sister, who moved to Boulder from Chicago and deeply enriched our Boulder IFS community.

As a psychotherapist and a coach, I have struggled with how to tell these stories and not reveal too much about my clients or retreat attendees. The names have all been changed, and their stories have been told as best as I can remember them. But the impact that these women have had on me is profound, and I continue to grow my own compassion quotient through witnessing women empowering women. I am deeply grateful to the women who have taken these journeys with me and opened themselves so they could grieve, rebirth, and explore these five stages on the midlife voyage all the way to the end. I want to thank Susie Kincade for her gifts and loving offerings along the way as we created these amazing retreats together.

I want to thank my Insight Meditation teachers of the Theravadan Buddhist tradition in Boulder and other MBSR and MSC teachers on my mindfulness path. I am especially grateful to Terry Ray for her early guidance, the inspiration to do women's retreats, and for how her retreats provided the experiences I needed to grow to become the retreat leader I am today. Johann Robbins, David Chernikoff, and Peter Williams, I am so grateful for your inspiration and guidance as my dharma teachers and spiritual teachers. This year especially, I want to thank Kritee Kanko for her support and spiritual guidance on the Zen path. I'm especially grateful to Janet Solynges, whose teaching and openheartedness greatly inspired me to become an MBSR teacher.

I am especially grateful to my special teachers and friends in the Christian UCC traditions in Boulder, both at the CUCC and First Congregational Church where I have served and been served. I want to thank Joanne Buchanan Brown for her powerful gift to me of spiritual direction over the past four years, but more importantly, for her powerful mirroring and love.

I am deeply grateful to my Florida family and their love and support through the years. I love being the second oldest of seven siblings and the power that position holds. I learned so much from my father's rugged entrepreneurship in citrus and my mother's deep compassion for so many, as well as her leadership with women. Our experiences with nature as a family have shaped me into the woman I am today, living and cherishing Colorado's beauty. I have treasured being a part of this large and wonderful family and its legacies, some of which I hope I have left behind, many which I am carrying forward proudly. We have many stories together, especially of the death of our sister Marjorie and its powerful impact on all of us. That event awakened me deeply to the immediacy of death and life, and it began my inner journeying. I am so grateful for my remaining two sisters, Ellen and Martha, who gave deeply to fill up that chasm in all our lives and with whom I have enjoyed great connections and support through these years.

I want to thank my son Julian for his great insight and patience in reviewing this manuscript, correcting where I needed his input and agreeing to this way of serving others by writing about our lives. I have had so many opportunities for learning in our relationship through the years, but the most powerful has been these past eight years that we have grown closer as adults on the path of life. I am so grateful for Julian's creativity and wisdom, generosity, patience, and loving presence. And most especially, his music. He continues to teach me so much.

I am exceedingly grateful to John Plock for his devoted love and understanding about the importance of this project to my life's work and for his willingness to begin again with me in a life together in our mid-sixties.

About the Author

DONNA ROE DANIELL, LCSW, is a family therapist, Certified IFS Therapist, life coach, meditation teacher, and retreat leader. She recently retired from her psychotherapy practice in Boulder, Colorado, after twenty-five years so she can focus on creating more adventure retreats, trips, and mindfulness retreats for women in midlife transitions.

Throughout her years in practice, Donna has treated children and families with special needs, couples, adoptive families, teens, and families dealing with divorce and death. Her practice shifted to an integrative focus with group classes to support treatment for families and women, and she ultimately developed a specific coaching program for women in midlife transitions. She has training in other trauma therapies besides Internal Family Systems (IFS) Therapy including Eye Movement Desensitization Reprocessing (EMDR), Somatic Attachment Training, and Somatic Experiencing (SE), and she has had a two-hundred-hour yoga training in the Anusara tradition. She has completed training to be a mindfulness-based stress reduction (MBSR) and Mindful Self-Compassion (MSC) teacher. She holds a MSW from Denver University and a BA in English from Vanderbilt University.

Donna's love of outdoor experiences grew when her family traveled to Alaska camping in a school bus for sixty-nine days in 1968. This experience ignited her desire to move to Colorado to learn to snow ski and climb mountains. Climbing rock pitches in Steamboat Springs and Boulder areas quickly grew into hiking and extended backpacking adventures. She has climbed almost all of the Fourteeners in Colorado and has guided with Timberline Adventures, a local outdoor adventure travel company. Donna leads nature-based mindfulness and adventure retreats at the Rocky Mountain Ecodharma Center outside Boulder and in other locations.

She lives with her life partner, John Plock, in their home in Longmont

Want to know more about Donna Roe Daniell and Women-in-Transformation?

JOIN A RETREAT

Adventure Retreats

Adventure Retreats offer 4 days and 3 nights of experiential learning with a small group of women doing mini-challenges—adventurous outdoor activities that are designed to move you past your comfort zone to help you feel yourself expanded beyond where you normally live within yourself. We offer support that empowers you to fully actualize your strengths, and we teach mindfulness and other self-care tools that bring in more self-love and deep connection with yourself and others. These retreats jump-start your healing, grow your resilience, and develop your capacity to choose what is right for you now in your life. You can learn about the upcoming Adventure Retreats at https://women-in-transformation.com/womens-retreats/or email donna@women-in-transformation.com or call 303 682-5220.

Women's Mindfulness Retreats

Women's Mindfulness Retreats offered by Women in Transformation are available through the Rocky Mountain Ecodharma Retreat Center (REMERC) near the foothills of Boulder, Colorado, and at other locations. These 4 day/3 night retreats offer guided mindfulness and self-compassion meditation training where you can experience the rejuvenation and healing that comes from deep immersion in nature. We use the

land, river, and the lodge during the fall season in the Rocky
Mountains to experience the healing practices of mindfulness
and we use the Internal Family Systems roadmap to heal grief
and trauma. These retreats are more spiritual in nature and
may evoke the call to serve more in the world. More information about this year's Mindfulness Retreats is available at
https://women-in-transformation.com/womens-retreats/
or you can call 303 682-5220 or email donna@women-in-
transformation.com.

SPEAKING ENGAGEMENTS, FACILITATION, AND LIVE WORKSHOPS

Donna is an inspiring speaker and workshop leader. She is
available to provide programs that empower women with a
variety of topics, and she can facilitate large or small groups.
Go to www.women-in-transformation/talks for information
or contact her at donna@women-in-transformation.com
or call 303 682-5220.

ONLINE OFFERINGS

The Midlife Voyage to Transformation Course, Meditations for
each of the Five Stages of the Midlife Voyage to Transformation
and other guided meditation and self-compassion offerings
that support your healing are available at https://women-in-
transformation.com/products/.

What clients are saying about Donna's retreats and coaching using the 5-Step Voyage to Transformation:

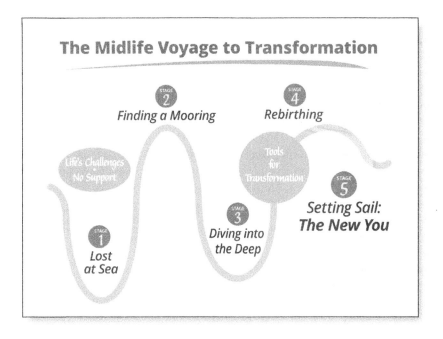

The Midlife Voyage to Transformation

STAGE 2 — *Finding a Mooring*

STAGE 4 — *Rebirthing*

Life's Challenges No Support

Tools for Transformation

STAGE 5 — *Setting Sail: The New You*

STAGE 3 — *Diving into the Deep*

STAGE 1 — *Lost at Sea*

I see both my marriage and my son's life through different lenses that I earned by going on the voyage with Donna. On this healing voyage, I learned so much about myself and how to be mindful. My life is by no means perfect, but I feel that I have reclaimed a part of myself that was lost for so long. I am also grateful to Donna for introducing me to the art of self-compassion. Bringing self-compassion meditations into my daily routine was instrumental in helping me learn to be kind and gentle with myself as I untangle years of living a life of perfectionism and simply demanding too much of myself.

–BARBARA Age 56

When I met Donna at a Women-in-Transformation retreat,
I was lost and confused in many facets of my life. I was experiencing
daily anxiety, stress, and uncertainty in my relationships with my
mother and my partner/spouse at the time. Through the retreats
and the individual IFS coaching with Donna, I learned about putting myself first, self-care, loving kindness, accepting myself as I am,
and setting healthy boundaries. All this work has freed me from the
fear and negativity that was crippling me. Releasing this negativity,
redefining relationships and knowing who I really am as a woman
have allowed me to begin an entirely new chapter of my life!

   –KRISTA Age 45

Through my own sorrow with Mom dying this winter, I am realizing
that I needed her but knew she was only halfway there with her
love and the way she used me. My internal parts, my exiles, don't
have to be used or denied any longer. I have learned how to manage
this event, my husband's heart attack, and other transitions in my
life the past ten years because of the tools of IFS and mindfulness
that I learned from coaching work with Donna and from attending
two of her retreats. I use mindfulness every day to keep myself
living positively and clear.

   –DONNA Age 61